Daughters of Hope

STORIES OF WITNESS

AND COURAGE

IN THE FACE

OF PERSECUTION

KAY MARSHALL STROM & MICHELE RICKETT

IVP Books
An imprint of InterVarsity Press
Downers Grove, Illinois

InterVarsity Press
P.O. Box 1400, Downers Grove, IL 60515-1426
World Wide Web: www.ivpress.com
E-mail: email@ivpress.com

InterVarsity Press® is the book-publishing division of InterVarsity Christian Fellowship/USA®, a student movement active on campus at hundreds of universities, colleges and schools of nursing in the United States of America, and a member movement of the International Fellowship of Evangelical Students. For information about local and regional activities, write Public Relations Dept., InterVarsity Christian Fellowship/USA, 6400 Schroeder Rd., P.O. Box 7895, Madison, WI 53707-7895, or visit the IVCF website at <www.intervarsity.org>.

All Scripture quotations, unless otherwise indicated, are taken from the Holy Bible, New International Version®. NIV®. Copyright ©1973, 1978, 1984 by International Bible Society. Used by permission of Zondervan Publishing House. All rights reserved.

Photo credits: Gayle Robinette Wafrock, Rachel Johnston, Lisa Ringnalda and Kay Strom

Cover design: Cindy Kiple

Cover image: Dennis Galente/Getty Images

ISBN-10: 0-8308-2366-2
ISBN-13: 978-0-8308-2366-6

Printed in the United States of America ∞

Library of Congress Cataloging-in-Publication Data

Strom, Kay Marshall, 1943-
   Daughters of hope: stories of witness & courage in the face of
persecution / Kay Marshall Strom and Michele Rickett.
     p. cm.
Includes bibliographical references.
   ISBN 0-8308-2366-2 (pbk.: alk. paper)
    1. Christian women—Developing countries—Biography. 2.
Persecution—Developing countries—History. 3. Christian
biography—Developing countries. I. Rickett, Michele, 1952- II.
Title.
   BR1608.5.S77 2003
   305.4′092′2—dc21

2003010875

P 24 23 22 21 20 19 18 17 16 15 14 13 12 11 10 9 8

Y 22 21 20 19 18 17 16 15 14 13 12 11 10 09 08 07

"An outcast Indian woman who suffered harsh persecution for her faith asked incredulously, 'If it doesn't cost you anything, how do you in America know what it means to be a Christian?'

After reading the poignant stories Kay and Michele tell of the persecuted women of faith around the world, I asked myself that question. I wept as I read of the Nigerian woman whose husband was killed the night Muslims burned their church, or the Sudanese mother raped and killed by the authorities, or the young Moroccan believer who escaped after her father threatened to kill her. They persevered because they love Jesus.

It's in these dark and difficult places of the world that women of God are demonstrating the reality of what it means to be a Christian. The heartbreaking stories awakened my heart, as they will yours, to seek justice, to pray for mercy and to thank God for the grace I so undeservedly enjoy."

LORRY LUTZ, AUTHOR OF *WOMEN AS RISK TAKERS FOR GOD* AND *WOMEN FINISHING WELL*

"This much-needed book provides compelling stories of the power of the kingdom of God in the lives of women suffering under the tyranny of injustice and oppression. Anyone reading this through the eyes of Christ will be motivated to take seriously the practical prayer and action steps suggested to help ordinary women become extraordinary witnesses in situations seemingly without hope."

JAMES F. ENGEL, RETIRED MISSIONS EDUCATOR, WRITER AND CONSULTANT

"*Daughters of Hope* is an eye-opening collection of stories about courageous women who are putting their lives on the line every day to spread the gospel of Jesus Christ. Kay Marshall Strom and Michele Rickett have done a wonderful job of representing these women and presenting, in a very riveting way, the dangers they face on a regular basis. Not only does it challenge the reader, but it also provides practical ways to become involved. I recommend it as a must-read for everyone who wants to know what God is doing in the most difficult-to-evangelize places in the world and how they can have a part in spreading the good news."

BEV CAREY, PRESIDENT, EVANGELICAL WOMEN, PACIFIC CONFERENCE OF THE EVANGELICAL CHURCH, EVANGELICAL CHURCH OF NORTH AMERICA

"In their book *Daughters of Hope* Michele and Kay have challenged my thinking. This book is filled with stories of ordinary women who have surrendered their lives to Christ and allowed him to use them to accomplish his purpose. They are his servants, showing us how to live out the truth of Colossians 3:3, 'For you died, and your life is now hidden with Christ in God.' Each story is different; the common thread is how God uses lives fully devoted to him."

DIANE JOHNSON, DIRECTOR OF WOMEN'S MINISTRIES,
MIDLAND EVANGELICAL FREE CHURCH, MIDLAND, MICHIGAN

"If you want to understand the reality of God working in and through the lives of thousands of women across the developing world today, then read *Daughters of Hope*. The power of story is undeniable, and the true stories you find here will bring you understanding as well as deeply move you."

JANE OVERSTREET, PRESIDENT/CEO,
DEVELOPMENT ASSOCIATES INTERNATIONAL

Contents

Acknowledgments 7

Introduction: *Our Sisters in the Hard Places* 9

PART 1: SOUTH ASIA

INDIA 23

    1 Marked for Freedom: *Sharmila's Story* 26

    2 Lowered for Love: *Rupali's Story* 33

PAKISTAN 39

    3 As for Me and My House: *Fouzia's Story* 42

PART 2: EAST ASIA

CHINA 51

    4 Greater Love Has No One: *Gong Mai's Story* 55

    5 Beautiful Feet: *Zhang Yuan's Story* 60

    6 China Trainer: *Polly's Story* 65

MACAO 69

    7 From the Rooftops to the Mountains: *Mrs. Chen's Story* . . 71

MONGOLIA 74

    8 The Long Journey: *Ye-Ling's Story* 76

PART 3: NORTH AFRICA

SENEGAL 83

    9 The Name of Jesus: *Songa's Story* 85

    10 Drawn by the Spirit: *Justine's Story* 88

ALGERIA 92

    11 "Dear Madame . . .": *Tanina's Story* 94

MOROCCO 99
   12 Put Your Hope in God: *Mehdi's Story* 101

TUNISIA 106
   13 A Lamp to My Feet and a Light to My Path: *Taiza's Story* . 108

SUDAN 112
   14 Mourning into Dancing: *Anna Lidu's Story* 114

PART 4: THE MIDDLE EAST

EGYPT 125
   15 By Their Fruit You Will Know Them: *Habiba's Story*. . . . 128
   16 Choosing the Hard Road: *Adel's Story* 132
   17 Though It Cost Me My Life: *Zora's Story* 136

PALESTINE 140
   18 The Baker's Daughter: *Randa Alea's Story*. 142

PART 5: THE MOST DANGEROUS PLACES ON EARTH

INDONESIA 151
   19 To Live Is Christ, to Die Is Gain: *Mirah's Story* 153

IRAQ 158
   20 With Love to Iraq: *Zadah's Story* 160

AFGHANISTAN 165
   21 Tell Me the Stories of Jesus: *Bahirah's Story* 167

NIGERIA 169
   22 Under Grace, Not Under Law: *Amaka's Story* 171

NORTH KOREA 175
   23 How Can They Hear? *Park Choi's Story* 177

How Shall We Then Live?. 184

Acknowledgments

To the many who contributed to this book, we gratefully extend our deepest appreciation. Partners International introduced us to several of their partner ministries around the world and allowed us to use their resources to facilitate many of our engagements. Without their extensive network and gracious collaboration, this book would not have been possible.

We had a wonderful team of traveling women—and one gentle man, Dan Kline. Thank you, Rachel Johnston, Stacie Bagley, Cherylann Sammons, Tina Lowe and Beverly Carey. Photographers Gayle Robinette Wafrock and Lisa Ringnalda brought fresh insight and perspective far beyond what the two of us could have captured. Our traveling companions celebrated, laughed, cried and prayed with us, mile after weary mile. What blessed and enriching company!

Our husbands, Daniel Rickett and Dan Kline, lovingly encouraged us to make the commitment of time and travel even in the most uncertain of times. Their generosity was a clear demonstration of faith and faithfulness to this important work.

We also gratefully acknowledge the churches and individuals that partnered with us in financial support and faithful prayer. From the beginning, Christ Presbyterian Church of Santa Barbara, California, was a particular champion of this project and was used by God to help make it possible.

The women we interviewed, who risked their personal safety and security in order to share their stories with us, are indelibly imprinted on our hearts and will forever be in our prayers. For their safety, the stories of most of these courageous Christians must be told with names altered. It has been our great privilege to tell the stories they entrusted to us, for the glory and honor of our Savior, Jesus Christ.

Introduction

OUR SISTERS IN THE
HARD PLACES

$\mathcal{W}$e were sitting on our hotel room beds in Hong Kong. Our trip was almost over. Early the next morning we would be catching a flight to Tokyo and another from there to Los Angeles.

"We need to talk about our experiences," we said to each other. "We have to get everything down on paper."

The tape recorder had stopped working a week before while we were talking to women alongside a dusty road in Hyderabad, India. Those had been our last interviews before the all-night layover in the Mumbai (Bombay) airport on our way to China. But it didn't much matter. We couldn't have recorded in China anyway. We couldn't even take real notes there for fear the authorities would confiscate them and use them to implicate the Christian women we were interviewing. Everything had to be written in a cryptic code that we ourselves could hardly decipher.

Our plan had been to get together with Cherylann, Rachel, Stacie, Gayle and Tina—the other members of our group—during the boat ride to the island of Macao, pool our recollections of who said what in China, and get it all down on paper. But the winds were blowing hard, and the water was so rough and choppy that everyone around us was seasick. We had spent the time praying with all our might that we would be able to keep it together and survive that miserable trip.

"We *must* get the stories down before we forget them," we agreed.

But we were exhausted. By the time we arrived home the following day, we would have made eighteen flights in seventeen days. We had sat with women in three cities in India and two cities in China and on the

islands of Hong Kong, Macao and Singapore. We had eaten more unfamiliar food than we cared to recall, we had struggled to find drinkable
water on three continents, and we had fought off hordes of mosquitoes,
remembering that we had stopped taking antimalaria pills because they
made us feel bad. Our insides were rumbling, our brains were spinning,
and we were weary beyond belief. And we still had North Africa and
Egypt to go.

The two of us flopped across our beds and lay in silence awhile. But
our minds would not let us rest. We began to recall the people we had
met and relive the experiences of the previous two-and-a-half weeks.

"Remember Wu Chein?" Michele asked.

*Wu Chein was just a child during China's Cultural Revolution, those
dark years when intellectuals and people of social standing were targeted
for reprogramming and families were ripped apart. Diffusion of power, it
was called. Deconstruction of the old order. Traditional families were
holding young people back, Chairman Mao insisted. The Communist
Party was to be the real family.*

*The last time Wu Chein saw her parents, her father was kneeling, head
bowed, with a sign around his neck that read: "I am a traitor." Her mother
was crying because Wu Chein's brother had just announced he had
joined the Red Guards and because ten-year-old Wu Chein, her school
closed, was being taken away to work in the far-off countryside.*

*"Life was so hard," Wu Chein said. "I worked for twelve hours a day,
and there was little food. The people didn't really want another hungry little girl there. My world was all loss and suffering."*

*Having been raised in an atheistic society, Wu Chein had no knowl-
edge of God. "I thought there surely must be a Creator," she said. "But I
couldn't find one."*

*When she was fourteen, Wu Chein's search for a Creator led her to em-
brace Buddhism. But to her great disappointment, her feelings of loss and
suffering remained. "My hope was gone," she said. "I decided there was
nothing left but to end my life."*

And so she began to watch for an opportunity.

There was an older woman on the farm who endured great abuse from the others. For some reason, Wu Chein confided her plans to her. The woman looked around to see who might be watching, then lowered her voice to a whisper and said, "Your problem, Wu Chein, is that you haven't found the true Creator. May I introduce you to him?"

"I was attracted to Jesus Christ by hope," Wu Chein told us, "but I was drawn to him by love. That is because I had no hope and I had never before felt love."

In the years after Chairman Mao, as the Cultural Revolution waned, Wu Chein made her way back to the city. Both her parents had died, and she was never able to locate her brother. She wanted to become involved with other believers, but she saw how they suffered for Christ and she was afraid. Two years passed before she gathered her courage to approach some Christians and tell them she wanted to join with them. Today she is a leader in a registered house church of more than one hundred people— three-quarters of them women, just as in most Chinese house churches.

Recalling Wu Chein's story was wonderful. It revived us more than a night's rest ever could. Other stories began flooding our minds.

"I'll never forget Pastor Esther Nayanthi in India," Kay said with a sigh.

Esther had graduated from a school of theology in northern India, but she declined an offer to live and work in that area. Instead she chose to work in southern India, in a village of people so desperately poor they could pay her only a handful of rice each week. Most of the men had left to find work in the city. The village was made up of those who had nowhere to go—starving women, children and old people who struggled to work the rice fields for a landlord who despised Christians.

"The landlord threatened the people, telling them he would have a curse put on them," Pastor Esther said. "But it didn't work. They believed in Jesus now, and they were no longer afraid of the landlord's curses."

In a final attempt to intimidate them, the landlord brought in a huge

Hindu idol and erected it in the middle of the village, right next to the small thatched church.

"I told them to ignore it and just go about their lives," Pastor Esther said. "It was just a piece of wood. It could not hurt us."

Before we left, Pastor Esther asked us to pray that the landlord would not burn the church down.

Now we knelt by our beds and prayed for the people of Pastor Esther's village.

A BATTLE RAGES

In all the world's hard places, it is women who suffer the most. And among those who struggle to see the kingdom of God advance and who are persecuted for the name of Jesus, women often pay a heavier price. Why must this be so? In our effort to understand, we turn to God's Word and discover where it all started—in the beginning.

After God created the heavens and the earth, the sea and dry land, the animals and the first man, God set to work on his grand finale. God's final creative gift to the man and to the world was a woman. She would be a strong partner, a completion for Adam and all humankind. According to the Creator, it simply was not good for man to be alone.

But something terrible happened when the man and woman sinned. Death and destruction began to work throughout every aspect of creation. Man would earn his daily bread by the sweat of his brow, and his special treasure, woman, would become the target of a great war. God warned of what was coming: "I will put enmity between you [the serpent] and the woman" (Genesis 3:15).

That war continues to this day. Eighty percent of the victims of war are women and children. So are 80 percent of refugees and displaced persons. Two million girls undergo mutilating circumcisions each year, and one quarter of them die as a result. The killing of infant girls in China and India has left entire villages without young women of marriageable age. In Indochina and Sudan, women and girls are sold into the sexual slave trade. Because from birth girls are not valued, meat and protein are not wasted on them, and so their bodies are not able to thrive. They are not educated, so their cognitive skills remain underdeveloped. Two-thirds of the world's illiterate people are women. And most tragic of all, 80 percent of the people who are unreached with the good news of God's love in Christ are women and children.

One of the greatest weapons in the arsenal of the woman's great adversary has been the prevailing views of religious teachers. Throughout the great religions of the world, there persist teachings that the woman is subhuman, a tool of Satan by which men are led astray. Jewish rabbis and Christian teachers have not been immune to such twisting of truth. Historically they too have been far too quick to devalue God's precious creation. But rather than quote them, let's look at what the Creator himself has to say.

THE GOOD NEWS

God's pronouncement to the serpent did not end with the enmity between him and the woman. The day would come, he said, when the woman's offspring "will crush your head, and you will strike his heel" (Genesis 3:15). Eve had no way of knowing that this prophecy would one day be fulfilled in Jesus Christ, God's own Son, born of a woman. And yet today Eve's daughters—women like Wu Chein and the believers at Pastor Esther Nayanthi's church—are finding hope and fulfillment in him.

For women who have been trampled down by society and the teachings of religious leaders, it is amazing to hear about a God who knows and deeply cares about them personally. Imagine how they respond when they hear what the Bible teaches about women: that they are created in the image of God (Genesis 1:27), that they are redeemed in Christ to be joint heirs to share in God's glory for all eternity (Romans 8:17), that the value of a woman is far above rubies and precious jewels (Proverbs 31:10), that before God there is no male or female (Galatians 3:28).

Women around the world are hearing the good news of Jesus Christ and are being drawn to God, their Creator, Redeemer and Abba Father. Today fully three-quarters of all Christians live outside the West. We have sisters and brothers in every one of the 189 countries that make up the United Nations.

We are family. It's time we get acquainted.

MODERN-DAY BATTLES

"Persecution? In this day and age?"

Most Westerners are shocked to learn that right now, in the twenty-first century, Christians are being punished and persecuted for simply being Christians. And when these believers dare to reach out and share the love of Christ with others, their suffering increases.

When American women recently heard some stories of their faraway sisters who struggle and suffer to serve God, we saw that they cared. They really did. And they were ready to take action.

"We want to know," they said. "And we want you to give us stories we can use to inform others."

"We believe in the power of prayer," others told us. "Let us know what to pray for specifically, and we will commit ourselves to a prayer ministry."

"We want to *do* something!" many women pleaded. "But we need to know where to start. Give us action points and turn us loose!"

That set us to thinking. In many ways we too felt clueless and helpless. We needed opportunities to sit down with women who were living in the trenches and listen to what they had to say. Not advise. Not teach or instruct. Just listen.

So we made some contacts through Sisters In Service[1] and Partners

---

[1]The focus of Sisters In Service (SIS) is extending the gospel to women and children in the least-reached places of the earth, through partnering relationships with local Christian leaders in Africa, China, India, the Middle East and Southeast Asia. SIS works to inform and mobilize those who have abundant resources to invest in local efforts that creatively and effectively extend God's love.

International.[2] We knew these organizations could put us in touch with women in the hardest places in the world. We rounded up a few hardy souls who were willing to join us, we packed our bags, and we went. Besides the locations in India, China and the nearby islands, the two of us took another trip—this time accompanied by Kay's husband and daughter, Dan Kline and Lisa Ringnalda—to Senegal, Tunisia, Morocco and Egypt. There were other countries from which we gathered stories in various ways. In all cases we have changed names and identifying details to protect the women and their ministries. But the stories recorded are the true stories of our sisters who live and serve in some of the most inhospitable places on earth for Christians.

In India, on our very first stop, when we told a group of women that we had come to listen to their stories, one stared at us and then commented, "When North Americans come here, they are always up on the stage telling us things. They only want to teach us. Are you really here to listen to us?"

We really were.

We had left on the first leg of our trip just months after the infamous September 11 terrorist attack on the Twin Towers in New York. That we Americans had had a taste of life under the pain and threat of terrorism on our own soil helped us feel even more connected to people for whom this was a way of life. Though our lives remained infinitely more secure than theirs, we were able to relate to hostility and the fear of uncertainty in a way we could not have just a few months earlier.

And it helped us to be more teachable.

"You in America really must study the teachings of Jesus about loving your enemies and doing good to those who want to hurt you," our sisters in China admonished us.

---

[2]Partners International "works to create and grow communities of Christian witness in partnership with God's people in the least Christian regions of the world." Founded in 1943 to assist Chinese evangelists, Partners International now works with eighty-five indigenous ministries in fifty-six countries to grow and strengthen the church through holistic witness in acts of service and proclamation. (Statement comes from Partners International's website: <www.partnersintl.org>.)

The more we saw and the more stories we heard, the more we determined to stand up for our sisters in the hard places.

When we were in India, we invited a shy woman from the Dalit (Untouchable) caste to tell us her story. She slowly lifted her eyes until she was looking us full in the face and stared at us in wonder. With tears running down her cheeks, she said, "No one has ever wanted to hear anything I had to say. And you came all the way from America to hear my story?"

Yes. For there is great power in a story. A story has the ability to draw us in, then grip our heart and turn us until we are changed forever. Especially when it is a story that pours from the depths of another's soul.

A TALE OF TWO WOMEN

"I am the mother of three daughters and no sons," Najma told us. "Cursed, that's what everyone called me. My husband is a Hindu, and he wanted me to abandon the second girl, but I would not. When the third girl came, he insisted that I get rid of her, but I refused. I am a Christian and I could not let my girls go, no matter how much my husband and his family beat me."

Girls brought the family no status, they brought in no money, and for a family as destitute as Najma's, the cost of the dowry required to marry a daughter off would be staggering.

The family began saving toward the first daughter's dowry the day she was born. But there was no money to put away for the second or third daughters.

When Najma's first daughter came of marrying age, they used all their savings to get her a husband. "He wasn't much of a husband," she said. "He was a drunkard and he didn't work much—but we got her a husband."

When Najma's second daughter came of marrying age, there was no money left. So Najma and her husband sold their house and all their belongings to pay a dowry. "Her husband was not as good as the first daugh-

ter's," Najma told us. "He was a drinker too, and he was also old and lame. He couldn't work at all. But at least she had a husband so she could work. Here a woman has to have a husband. Otherwise she has no one to take care of her, and she can only be a prostitute."

Then Najma fell silent.

"What about the third daughter?" we asked.

In a voice so soft we could hardly hear, she said, "When my third daughter came of marrying age, we had no money and nothing left to sell. So my daughter threw herself into a fire and died. She had to do it. There was no other way."

We sat in stunned silence.

There had to be another way! Najma was a believer in Jesus Christ. How could she have valued her daughters' lives enough to resist tradition despite all the punishment and abuse her husband's family heaped upon her, then resign herself to her youngest's suicide?

For the next several days, we listened to many stories from many Indian women. Most of them, like Najma, had come out of Hinduism, and almost all were poor and from the untouchable Dalit caste. Their stories were touching and inspiring and sometimes painful to hear. Amid them all, we could not get Najma's story out of our minds.

Then came Ivy.

"I am the mother of three daughters and no sons," Ivy began. "My family said I should not keep all those girls, but I said, 'I will not abandon my daughters. They are a gift from God. Even if you beat me, I still will not let them go.'"

Like Najma, Ivy saved enough for her first daughter's dowry. And like Najma, she had to sell everything she owned to afford a husband for her second daughter. But her situation was even worse: her Hindu husband deserted her and the youngest daughter and left them to fend for themselves.

We braced ourselves for the story's ending.

"And my third daughter was coming to marrying age, so I could do only *one thing—I could only trust God. I prayed and she prayed. We prayed together. I told my daughter not to fear, that the Lord God of heaven would hear our prayers. Every morning when we awoke and every night when we lay down, we would pray Psalm 61: 'Hear my cry, O God; attend unto my prayer. From the ends of the earth will I cry unto thee, when my heart is overwhelmed; lead me to the rock that is higher than I. For thou hast been a shelter for me, and a strong tower from the enemy. . . .'"*

"And what happened?"

"I got a job at the Bible Faith Mission," she said. "I earned money for my daughter's dowry."

The third daughter alone, of the three, is married to a Christian man. Today the young couple is preparing for the ministry.

ONE BODY

We North Americans find it hard to understand the challenges of balancing cultural constraints with the value of human life and personal rights that we take for granted. Any persecution we have suffered for our faith is not even close to what many of our sisters have undergone. Can we truly empathize with Ivy? Or Najma? Or Wu Chein? Or our sisters in Algeria or Palestine or Iraq or Nigeria or Sudan or Egypt?

We can, because we are all one body. Since the same nerves run through all of us, if one of us suffers, we all suffer. According to 1 Corinthians 12:23-26, that's how it is. If we are not suffering with our sisters and brothers, then something is wrong. The body is not functioning the way it should be.

Imagine our surprise when we found that our sisters in hard places identified with *us*. When we told Wu Chein we admired her for all she was willing to risk in order to live for Jesus Christ, she smiled and replied, "To live as true Christians, to be like the Master, is not easy anywhere. I am praying for you too."

Whatever your background or location, come meet some of your sisters from the hard places around the globe.

If you are part of a group that meets regularly—a Bible study or small group—consider going through the book together. Group members might read the stories ahead of time, then come together prepared for prayer and discussion. You might then decide to take one or more of the suggested action steps, either individually or together.

We are confident that you will be encouraged and inspired by the stories of these women, just as we have been. It is our prayer that you will also be called to action.

We can make a difference together. With our faraway sisters, we can reach around the world and empower each other in Jesus' name.

PART 1

South Asia

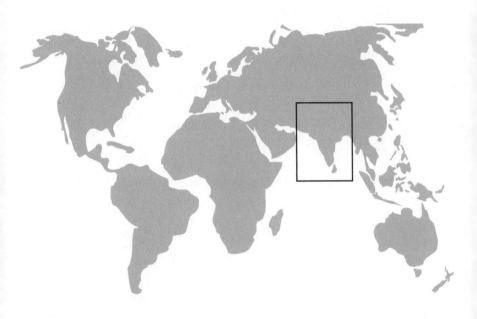

INDIA

Population: 1,045,845,226

Religion: 81.3% Hindu, 12% Muslim, 2.3% Christian, 1.9% Sikh

Adult Literacy: Male 65.5%, Female 37.7%[1]

Government: World's largest functioning democracy. Hindu extreme nationalist movements have grown in strength and influence. Many fear an undermining of democracy.

*I*t was 4:00 a.m. and we were wide awake. Peacocks were calling and monkeys were chattering, but what woke us were the chants from a nearby Hindu temple. Soon women would be busy in the kitchen below our window. Night was over.

We had been in India just one day, but we were already staggered by this country of one billion people crowded into an area one-third the size of the United States. Home to one of every six people on earth, it has the world's highest population density per square mile. Approximately 65 percent of Indian women are illiterate, and according to the World Health Organization, rural Indian women are the hardest-working people in the world. For centuries Indian women have suffered ex-

---

[1]Statistics for all countries come from Central Intelligence Agency, *CIA World Factbook 2002*, updated July 2002. Available at <www.cia.gov/cia/publications/factbook/index.html>.

ploitation and oppression. Today there is widespread abandonment and
killing of baby girls and a terrifyingly high suicide rate among women.

The most miserable of all are the outcasts of Indian society, the people formerly known as the "Untouchables," the lowest caste, the Dalits.
The Hindu doctrine of reincarnation teaches that people are born into
specific social strata. Those in lower castes are supposedly paying for
sins they committed in an earlier life. They are usually consigned to menial, degrading tasks and to a lifetime of poverty.

The Dalits face pervasive, humiliating and intense discrimination.
They are allowed only extremely limited educational opportunities.
Not surprisingly, they often lack self-esteem and initiative and tend to
keep their gaze downcast. One-third of India's population falls into
this category.

Because of outcry against the hopelessness of the Dalits' plight, India
has adopted a type of affirmative action: certain things are set aside for
Dalits in proportion to their numbers in the general population. The
benefits include jobs, government loans and university admissions, as
well as medical care, basic education and housing. The program attempts to begin to alleviate the wretchedness in which the untouchables have existed for centuries. Unfortunately, all religious groups are
eligible for this relief except one: Christians. The Indian government
explicitly excludes them. And over half—perhaps up to two-thirds—of
all thirty million Christians in India are Dalits.[2]

Indian Christians are often accused of undermining Hinduism and
the social order. In a way this is true. The Bible teaches that all human
beings are created in God's image, so the lowest Dalits have as much
value as members of the highest caste. This concept threatens the established social order. Most Indian Christians don't preach against the social order or organize against it, yet they are a threat merely because
they maintain that all people are equal in the eyes of God. Thus, at all

[2]Manpreet Singh, "Quitting Hinduism," *Christianity Today*, December 9, 2002, pp. 22-23.

costs, those in power feel compelled to keep the Christians down; otherwise members of the low castes may discover that they have value. Were that to happen, they might decide to rise to their full potential and refuse to remain subservient "untouchables." They might reject the caste system altogether.

Since 1990 more Christians have been martyred, raped, beaten and threatened in India than in the entire history of Christianity in that country. This is truly astounding, considering that Indian Christianity dates back to the first century when, as Christians there told us with great pride, the apostle Thomas came to tell the Indian people the good news of Jesus Christ and was martyred. New, oppressive restrictions against changing one's religion, or even talking to someone about changing religions, are sure to engender even more persecution and suffering.

Yet in India we heard stories of incredible perseverance, generosity and sacrifice.

1

Marked for Freedom

SHARMILA'S STORY

*S*harmila grew up struggling to appease the assortment of gods and goddesses her family worshiped. The family was desperately poor, and on many days after Sharmila's father and brothers finished eating there was barely enough food left for her mother. Because Sharmila and her sisters couldn't eat until everyone else had finished, they often went to bed aching with hunger. Yet the family always managed to scrape together enough money to buy offerings for the idols that stood in places of honor around their small hut. And gifts were taken to beautiful Hindu temples, each one honoring a different deity. Sharmila's family left their gifts of fruits, vegetables and flower necklaces by the statues in the temple courtyard, because Dalits were not allowed to enter the temples.

"When anyone from a higher caste came by, they did their best to keep their distance from us," Sharmila said. "If they came in contact with a Dalit they would become unclean. Then they would have to go through a ritual cleansing before they could go into the temple." Sharmila looked down as she spoke.

We asked what it was like to worship images made of wood and stone. "I was afraid of them," she said. "I knew they had great power to do terrible things if I didn't keep them happy. I always worried and wondered just what they wanted from me."

By the time Sharmila was ten years old, her father had saved enough to buy a gold bracelet to add to her dowry. But he hesitated to make the purchase, wanting to make sure the gods considered it a good day for jewelry buying. "He consulted the calendar," she told us. "He looked at the time the sun and moon rose and when they went down. Finally he made the purchase, but he still worried that he might have made a mistake."

When Sharmila came of marrying age, her family didn't have much to offer in the way of a dowry. At seventeen she was married to Ajay, a man who suffered from mental illness and so commanded only a small dowry. At first he was able to work a bit, but small provocations set him off and he would explode in anger. More and more often his anger led to violence. Sharmila begged her idols for help and protection. She prayed at home, and she also made trips to various temples with gifts she could not afford. Yet her husband grew steadily worse. When enraged, he began to grab her around the neck and choke her until she thought she would die.

Three years into their marriage, Ajay attacked someone at work. The authorities were called, and he was taken to a hospital in the city and locked up. Sharmila went to the hospital every Friday to see him and to take him food. He improved and was sent home.

For a while things went well, but before long Ajay became violent again. Finally, in fear for her life, Sharmila took her children and moved to her parents' house. Her father insisted the real problem was that the gods had not approved of the buying date of that gold dowry bracelet and were taking revenge. Ajay was returned to the hospital. Every Friday Sharmila left her children with her parents and made the long trip to the city to take food to her husband. Since she had to walk both ways, it took her most of the day.

One day a childhood friend came to visit her. "Sharmila," she said, "I have found someone who can tell me answers to my problems. I know you have hard problems. Will you come and hear what she says? Will you come to my Bible study with me?"

Sharmila's first thought was, *This will cost me money, and I don't have any!* So she told her friend no.

But her friend didn't give up. She came back the next night, bringing rice and a bit of chicken. She also had a Bible and a study guide on the Gospel of John. "Look," she told Sharmila, "I brought this so we could do the lessons together right here. It won't cost anything, and I can help you since I know how to read."

After that her friend came early every Friday morning. Together they walked to the hospital in the city; then they walked back and did the Bible study lesson in the evening. As they studied God's Word together, the Holy Spirit worked in Sharmila's heart. "The gods I had feared all my life frightened me no more," she told us. "I threw them out of my house and smashed them on the ground. I knew my mother and father would be furious with me, but I didn't care. Only one thing scared me, and that was that I would have to tell my husband I was now a follower of Jesus Christ. I didn't know what he would do. If he choked me to death, what would happen to my children? They would never know about the real God who loves them and died to take them to heaven."

"You don't have to tell him now," her friend urged. "Wait until he gets out of the hospital and comes home."

"But Jesus Christ could make him well," Sharmila argued. "How can I not tell him about the only true God who can change his life? I must tell him now!"

"Then I will go with you," her friend said.

The two women set off on the long, familiar walk. Suddenly her friend stopped. "Just for a change, let's go a different way," she said.

"Why?" Sharmila asked.

"I don't know. Wouldn't it be nice to see something different?"

Sharmila shrugged, and the two turned up a different road. Halfway to town, they saw a man walking toward them. As he came closer, Sharmila said, "That's my husband!"

"They sent him home even though he's still sick!" her friend exclaimed.

Sharmila's hand flew to her throat. "What will I do?"

"There will be people at the church tonight. Take him there for prayer," her friend suggested.

That night was especially dark, the night of the new moon. "A special day for demons, the Hindus say," Sharmila noted. Many pastors conduct special meetings on that night because of the superstitions. Sharmila, who had always been terrified of the dark, shivered with fear and dread all the way to church. But her husband was surprisingly quiet as she led him along the pitch-black road.

The church meeting lasted two hours, but Sharmila and Ajay stayed just long enough for the people to pray. Everything was going all right, and she wanted to avoid inciting her husband's wrath. She and Ajay walked most of the way back together, but when he turned off to go to their house, she had to make her way on to her parents' house alone.

By the time Sharmila got inside, everyone had gone to sleep. She turned on the one electric light, but within minutes the electricity went out. Once again she was plunged into darkness.

"Before I had time to be afraid, I saw a bright light come through the window. Then I felt something saying, 'Don't worry and don't be afraid. I am the God you are searching for. I was always with you even in your mother's womb. Even though you went and worshiped so many idols, I didn't leave you. I am the one true God and I am here.' Then the light disappeared."

The next morning, Sharmila ran to tell the pastor's wife what she had seen and heard. The pastor's wife turned to Luke 15:4-7 and read her the story of the shepherd who sought the one lost sheep and brought it back to the fold. "You are that lost sheep, Sharmila," she said. "God has sought you out." Then they knelt down and prayed together. And they prayed again for Ajay's healing.

When Sharmila got back to her parents' house, she told her mother and father that she was trusting Jesus Christ to heal her husband and protect her from harm. Then she packed her belongings and her children to move them back home.

Her parents, furious at her for forsaking the idols of her family, shouted threats against her and Ajay. As she left, they followed her down the road, yelling all the way.

Sharmila paused in her story.

"What happened?" we asked.

"My husband was healed," she said quietly. "He has no more mental illness. And when he saw that the Christian God—*my* God—could immediately do what all the more than 300 million Hindu gods hadn't been able to do throughout his entire life, he was ready to become a Christian too."

Despite the angry opposition and threats from their families, Sharmila and Ajay, along with their two children, began worshiping at the Christian church.

When we met Sharmila in Chennai, she had stood out from the other Christian women because she wore a *pottu*, a red mark in the middle of her forehead. Hindus consider this a sacred mark, but once a woman comes to Christ, it is almost always removed.

"Why do you wear it?" we asked her.

"Because I am not a widow," Sharmila explained.

This left us even more confused, since few of the other women were widows.

There was more to the story: shortly after Sharmila told her family of her conversion, her husband's family sent him a message. Should she stop wearing the sacred *pottu*, they warned, they would assume she considered herself separated from Ajay and they would kill her. Because of that death threat, Sharmila's pastor gave her permission to continue wearing the mark.

"The time will come when they will accept us, and then the *pottu* will go," Sharmila said. Then she added, "Or maybe we won't continue to wait."

"What is your life like today?" I asked Sharmila.

"Freedom because of Jesus!" she said with a big smile. "I save a little money so I can buy coconut or pineapple, but I give it to my children, not to idols!"

For the first time in his life, Ajay is able to earn enough to support his family. "We have a small shop that my husband runs, and every morning he prays before he goes to work. He asks for God's protection and that God will let him be a missionary that day. And he thanks God that he can work and take care of his family."

Most of their relatives are still Hindus. Only Sharmila's mother has become a Christian. "They are all amazed at what Jesus Christ did for Ajay," Sharmila said, "but even though they saw what happened with their own eyes, it takes time. They are afraid if they leave the gods our ancestors worshiped that something terrible will happen to them. I learned to read so I can teach Bible studies in my village, and I am praying that some of my family will come and study with me."

Besides leading Bible studies, Sharmila is mentoring eight new Christians. Like her, these women face crippling poverty and an oppressive culture, and because of their stand for Christ, they suffer beatings, threats and further discrimination at the hands of husbands and relatives.

Sharmila has very little in material goods. She lives under a death sentence from her parents-in-law. Yet she is busy spreading the gospel of Jesus Christ. She knows what it means to be free indeed!

Sharmila is one of the few Christians who has been granted permission by her pastor to continue wearing a *pottu*, a mark Hindus consider sacred and required of married women.
[Photo - Gayle Robinette Wafrock]

PRAYER POINT

Pray for Sharmila as she teaches and mentors the women in her village.
Pray that through her example and Ajay's, many will come to know the
Great Physician who can not only heal the body but also free the soul
from bondage.

2

Lowered for Love

RUPALI'S STORY

*T*all and willowy with a long, thin face and creamy skin, Rupali stood out among the stockier, darker Dalit women gathered around us. We had been told that all the women were Dalits and dark skin was one of their distinguishing characteristics. Why did Rupali look different?

A couple of the women who spoke broken English told us interesting facts about each of the others. When they got to Rupali, it sounded as if they said she had a "low marriage."

"A *low* marriage?" Kay asked.

The English speakers looked at each other and started to giggle. Then they said something to the others, who also reacted with amusement. Obviously there was something we were missing.

"*Low* marriage!" the best English speaker said again.

Cautiously Kay repeated, "*Low* marriage?"

This time they laughed out loud. Rupali covered her face and laughed behind her hands. We gave up and motioned for the interpreter. Through peals of laughter, the women explained to her, and soon the interpreter was laughing as hard as the others.

"Although you don't understand," the interpreter explained, "you are right in what you say."

What the women had been trying to tell us was that Rupali was in a *love* marriage, a rare and wondrous thing in India. Nearly all marriages are arranged, and for a Dalit woman, whose dowry is small, the husband is usually a disappointment. But Rupali was from a higher caste and had done the unimaginable—she had married down into a low caste. For love, she had married an untouchable and in so doing had become an untouchable herself. For love, Rupali had married low.

Here is her story.

When Rupali was very young, her mother died. Her father then took responsibility for his sons but abandoned his only daughter. Why burden himself with a girl who would require the expenditure of a goodly sum of money for a dowry? Rupali's uncle took pity on the child and took her in.

When she was twelve, she and her cousin went to Sunday school with a friend. Rupali was very moved by the stories she heard about Jesus Christ, God's Son, and the good he did for people. And when the teacher told her this true God loved her, an abandoned girl, enough to give his life so that she could live forever in heaven with him, she was moved beyond words. She came back the next week and told the teacher she wanted to be a Christian.

When her uncle heard about it, he was filled with disgust. "A Christian?" he said. "And in a church with *untouchables?* You are an Indian, and all true Indians are Hindus. Don't you ever go back there again!"

When Rupali disobeyed his command and sneaked back to the church, he beat her and demanded she renounce Christianity. She refused, and he turned her out of his house, telling her she could never come back. At the age of twelve, Rupali was on her own—no home, no family, no dowry.

This was a terrible plight. There is little option for an Indian girl alone but to turn to prostitution. Rupali managed to survive by begging and by accepting handouts from people in the church, but the other Christians were careful to keep their distance from her. They knew they were not her social equals.

The church members watched with great curiosity, however, as Rupali fell in love with Dilawar, a Dalit who had been disowned by his family for becoming a Christian. When Rupali was sixteen, the two married. No one in the church had seen a love marriage before. And no one had ever before seen a high-caste girl willingly become an untouchable and take on all the accompanying degradation and humiliation.

Love for Christ had drawn Rupali to faith, even though it meant humbling herself and giving up the only family and security she knew. She found new love and acceptance in her husband and her church. But her faith was to face another challenge, one that came with being a believer who was a member of the lowest caste.

"One day my husband came home and told me he couldn't keep his job cleaning streets," Rupali said. "I asked him why, and he said it was because we were Christians. He had to give it up so a Hindu could have the job. Then he told me we would have to leave our house too. So we had no money and no house. We have no families, so we didn't have any place to go."

Rupali asked her husband, "Do the authorities want us to starve on the streets?"

"No," he told her. "They want us to be Hindus again."

Certainly they were not the only family facing this predicament. Some Dalit believers went to live with relatives, but many had unsympathetic Hindu families. And it was a poor area; no one could afford to feed extra hungry people. To her horror, Rupali watched as one family sold their young daughter into bonded servitude to provide a bit of money for the rest of the family to survive. With nothing to pay the master back, the child would spend her entire childhood in virtual slavery. Several other families gave up and returned to Hinduism.

In desperation, some Christians tried a different strategy. By masquerading as Hindus, they were able to accept the government benefits, yet they continued to worship secretly with fellow believers.

"Of all our choices, it's the best," Dilawar told Rupali. "We could have a house and I could get my job back. God will know what is in our hearts. Isn't that what really matters?"

Rupali was not convinced. Still, she didn't have any other ideas, so she reluctantly agreed.

Dilawar went to the magistrates to inform them that he and his wife had converted back to Hinduism. Although Rupali felt guilty before God about what they were doing, things did seem to be working out. Dilawar got his job back, and they got a house in their former neighborhood. But before long Rupali began to have the distinct feeling that they were being watched. Then without warning Dilawar's work schedule was rearranged so that he had to work on Sundays and could not go to church.

"We cannot do this," Rupali protested. "We must be honest about being Christians."

"But there is no other way for us to live," Dilawar told her.

Moses Swamidas, head of the Bible Faith Mission in Kerala, insists there must be another way. For years he has worked hard to get Christian Dalits included in government benefits. Until that happens, Bible Faith Mission has a program for people like Rupali and Dilawar.

Rupali's story reminds us of our Savior who came to earth and became low caste for us.
[Photo - Gayle Robinette Wafrock]

When Rupali first visited BFM, she could not even write her own name. There she was taught to read and write, and she took Bible classes. She was also encouraged to choose a trade skill that would allow her to earn a living; she chose mat weaving. After learning to organize and manage her own business, she was able to take out a small loan to help her buy the supplies she would need.

"Very soon I started to make some money," Rupali said. "And Dilawar just got a job working in a rice field, so I am starting to pay the loan back." As she does, that money will be made available to other women.

The program requires Rupali to save one rupee each week (one rupee equals two cents U.S.). That does not seem like much to us, but it teaches Indian women the process of saving and lending, it builds up their self-esteem, and it allows them to have small but growing accounts from which they can draw in cases of emergency.

"You must be so pleased to be a businesswoman now!" we said to Rupali.

She responded, "I'm most happy not to be pretending I'm not a Christian. Jesus didn't pretend. He stayed on earth and died on the cross for me."

We asked Rupali how, besides the obvious ways, her life had changed when she became a Dalit.

"Sometimes I am ashamed to be a higher caste," she said. "High-caste Christians don't treat Dalit Christians like brothers and sisters. They think that they deserve a lot more and better, that if Dalits come

These Dalit women have learned to read and write so that they can share God's Word with other women in their villages. [Photo - Gayle Robinette Wafrock]

to their churches they should have to stand in the back. But castes are not for Christians. They are for Hindus. The true God doesn't have untouchables."

PRAYER POINT

As you pray for the plight of the Dalits in India, praise God for our Savior Jesus Christ, who willingly left the realms of heavenly glory and became low caste in order to provide salvation for us.

PAKISTAN

Population: 147,663,429

Religion: 97% Muslim (77% Sunni, 20% Shi'a); 2.3% Christian, Hindu and other

Adult Literacy: Male 55.3%, Female 29%

Government: Federal republic

*O*n September 25, 2002, gunmen burst into the offices of the Institute for Peace and Justice, a Pakistani Christian charity in the city of Karachi. They bound the workers and taped their mouths. Then, one by one, they shot them point-blank in the head. Seven died that day.

Pakistan is not a hospitable place for Christians.

Concentrated mainly in the Punjab and in the port city of Karachi, most believers in Jesus Christ belong to the poorest stratum of Pakistani society, and that is where most of them will remain. Their educational opportunities are restricted, they are barred from holding certain professions, and the most menial jobs are reserved for them.

During the 1980s the climate grew even harsher for Pakistani Christians. At this writing, they are marginalized politically, forced to vote on separate electoral rolls. In court, a Christian man's testimony has only half the value of a Muslim's, and a Christian woman's only a quarter the value.

The nation's Blasphemy Law states that any insult to Islam or the Prophet Muhammad is a penal offense punishable by death. Though Muslims and Hindus also suffer under it, the very fact that this law exists promotes hostility against Christians and provides a perfect opportunity to take advantage of them. When someone goes to the police and accuses a person of blasphemy, the police must, by law, immediately arrest and jail the accused person. There need not be any proof, no witnesses are required, and no investigation need be conducted. And there is no possibility of bail for the accused.

Ayub Masih was arrested on October 14, 1996, after neighbors accused him of making derogatory statements against the Prophet of Islam and of suggesting they read Salman Rushdie's book *The Satanic Verses*. He was charged under the law, convicted and sentenced to death.

In July 2001 Masih's sentence was upheld by the High Court. He was placed on death row in a hot, dark cell with no light, no fan and no toilet. In a letter he said, "I am sick with various diseases and have not been allowed any medicines—my conditions are getting worse all the time."[1]

Masih's case caused an uproar both within and outside of Pakistan. Human rights leaders around the world called for his release—especially when his lawyer produced evidence showing that the case had little to do with blasphemy and much to do with a land dispute in his village. For six long years—longer than anyone else had been held on a blasphemy charge—Masih had managed to survive attempts on his life, regular torture and wracking illnesses. Amid death threats to him and his lawyer, he prepared to mount one last appeal from death row. Should that fail, he would be immediately hanged.

Christians around the world prayed for him, and he knew it. "I am a very humble servant of God who is now in jail," he wrote.

The three judges who presided over the appeal noted that the charge had been used by one of the accusers to acquire property belonging to Masih's family. All three were convinced that the charges had been fabricated so the neighbor could increase his holdings. On August 15, 2002, Ayub Masih was acquitted and ordered released.

---

[1]World Evangelical Alliance, Religious Liberty Prayer List 130, August 21, 2001.

When General Pervez Musharraf, president of Pakistan, suggested changing the law to require some investigation before an arrest in order to discourage false accusations, Islamic groups reacted so sharply that he quickly backed down.

3

As for Me and My House
FOUZIA'S STORY

It was early Friday morning, and the day was just beginning. The staff of the Christian missionary hospital were gathered in the chapel, asking God's blessing on the day. When the women—always the first to leave a building—headed out the door, terrorist attackers lobbed hand grenades at them. Three nurses were killed, and seventy other staff members were injured.

Fouzia's heart sank when she heard the news. "Another attack!" she exclaimed, and she sat down and cried. A hospital this time! And just outside of Islamabad, Pakistan's capital city.

Just days before, there had been an attack on a Christian school. Gunmen had killed six that day. Before that it was an attack on the Protestant International Church in Islamabad. Security forces were supposed to be guarding it, but somehow they had mysteriously disappeared by the time the attackers crept up and tossed hand grenades in on the worshiping Christians. Five died and forty were injured.

"We are targets, every one of us Christians!" Fouzia's sister had warned. "We must keep quiet about our faith. This is not the time to go to church, certainly not the time to take our children there. This is the time to be still and not call attention to ourselves."

"I cannot agree," Fouzia argued. "If we do not stand up for our God, then the terrorists have won."

"And what if they kill us all?" her sister asked. "Who has won then?"

Still, Fouzia gathered her children and walked them to worship every Sunday. "We are Christians," she told them. "We will not be afraid to say so."

But now this. Her sister would be at her door soon, telling her again what a fool she was.

Fouzia's oldest daughter was seventeen, just the age of another Christian teenager who, a few months before, dared to reject the sexual advances of a Muslim man. When he walked into the Public Call Office where that girl worked as a telephone operator and tried to fondle her, she slapped his face. The next day when she arrived at the office, the man walked up and threw acid in her face, taking care to splash her eyes and mouth.

"Are you frightened by this morning's bombing at the mission hospital?" Fouzia asked her daughter.

"Yes," her daughter said. "But no more than by all the other things . . ."

All the other things. Like the fourteen-year-old girl who was kidnapped from her home in the Shiekhupura district by Islamic extremists. One of them was angry because the girl had dared to speak of her faith in Jesus Christ to her schoolmates, one of whom was his daughter. So he rounded up his friends, and they kidnapped the young girl and brutally raped her. They told her they would let her go only if she converted to Islam. When she refused, they continued to torture her.

Or the two pastors' families who were helping eight Christian girls who had been raped by Islamic extremists and had dared to take their attackers to court. The judge determined there was insufficient evidence to go to trial, despite an entire vanload of eyewitnesses and medical reports that confirmed the rapes. The charges were dismissed. Despite this, the militants were infuriated at the girls. They broke into the pastors' homes and assaulted the women of the families, including one pastor's mother. "Stop supporting the girls," they ordered, "or we will come back and kill all of you!"

"It is hard for Christians to live in Pakistan," Fouzia said. "I know that. There are many militants, and they don't want us here. The Blasphemy Law is frightening to all of us. Anyone can use it against us, and there is nothing we can do. But it has always been this way. It has always been hard."

She fell silent. It was a while before she continued.

"Now, after the attack on the school and the hospital, everyone is once more in shock," she said softly. "We all feel sad."

And more afraid?

"And more afraid."

But even as she spoke, Fouzia was gathering her children to go to church.

"Maybe it will not be my enemies who will be watching me," she said. "Maybe it will be other Christians. Maybe when they see us going to worship God and to pray, in spite of what all is happening, in spite of our fears, they will be encouraged to come along and worship with us."

And what about the danger to herself and her family?

Fouzia simply said, "We will trust God."

As for me and my household, we will serve the LORD.
(Joshua 24:15)

PRAYER POINT

Remember our sisters and brothers who live under the constant threat of terrorist attack. Pray that those who see their faithfulness to Christ in the face of danger will have their hearts changed and turned to God.

South Asia

PRAYER POINTS

- In parts of India, a strong ordinance banning religious conversions by "force, allurements, or fraudulent means" was passed in 2002; it requires that all conversions be reported to local magistrates. Violators can be imprisoned for up to three years and fined up to fifty thousand rupees—but if the violator is a woman, her fine is much higher and her imprisonment term is extended to four years. Furthermore, anyone who converts to another religion must go before local authorities and explain the reasons for converting. Pray for India's new believers, most of them Dalits, and for the Christians who are discipling them.

- Pray for groups that are raising funds to enable poor Indian Dalit Christian women to find Christian men for life mates and to pay the required dowries.

- Pray for those whose vision is to persuade Indian Christians to opt out of the dowry system, an entrenched tradition that puts a terrible burden on the families of poor women.

- Pray for the Indian Dalit Christians. They live under all the stigma and pain of the untouchable status, yet they are excluded from the help the government offers to alleviate those pains. Pray that they will believe that through the power of God there is hope for change. Pray especially for the women, that they will be able to see themselves as beloved daughters of God, lovingly created in his image.

- Pray that Christians born into higher-caste Indian families will be able to supersede the limitations of tradition and see that all believers, whatever their caste, are truly their brothers and sisters, equals in every way.

- Remember Pakistani Christians who have been imprisoned on

charges of blasphemy. Pray that they will be protected from harm, disease and despair.

- Pray that there will be persistent pressure from the international community against Pakistan's Blasphemy Law. Pray that God will intervene and the law will be removed so that it can no longer be used for religious persecution.

- Helpful prayer tools can be found from a number of sources. Check out the Caleb Project website at <www.calebproject.org> or call 1-303-730-4170 for resources on various people groups. There are video prayer guide packets that can greatly inform your prayer life, along with an informative prayer calendar for children *(Kids Around the World)* and a children's version of *Operation World*, a prayer guide for the nations. For adults there is Patrick Johnstone's periodically updated *Operation World* (Carlisle, U.K.: Paternoster Lifestyle, 2001).

South Asia
ACTION POINTS

- The Indian government denies that the caste system still exists in India, although everyone knows that it does. It is part and parcel of Hinduism. Make yourself aware of the all-encompassing plight of the Dalits and be willing to speak out on their behalf.

- Create an advocacy team of women who will disperse information, speak up for and help Dalit and other Indian women and girls. Programs for Indian women are making a difference, but they require resources: Indian Christian leaders with boldness and initiative, financial investment and the sacrificial work of strong advocates.

- Our culture portrays Hinduism (along with Buddhism) as a benign, pacifist religion. Become acquainted with the truth of this religion, which is rooted in demonology, and be ready to challenge the prevalent misperceptions.

- Contact your senators and representatives and express concern for the well-being of Christians in Pakistan. Ask elected officials to make an inquiry into the status of those being held on charges stemming from the Blasphemy Law.

PART 2

East Asia

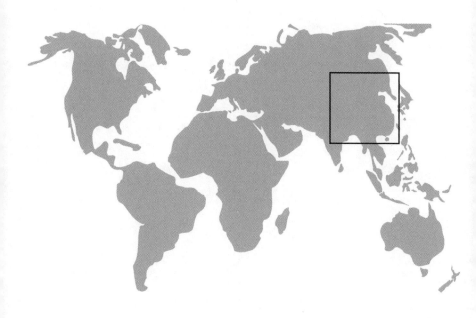

CHINA

Population: 1,284,303,705

Religion: Officially atheist; 4% Christian;
                  2% Taoist, Buddhist, Muslim

Adult Literacy: Male 89.9%, Female 72.7%

Government: Communist state

*O*ur Sisters In Service group was a week away from leaving for China when I (Kay) got a call from the company handling our visas. Mine was being challenged. Having discovered I was a writer of religious books, the Chinese officials were balking at allowing me entrance into the country. I got in, but it was a fight all the way. We experienced Chinese "religious freedom" before we even left home.

China is not only the oldest continuous major civilization but also the largest nation on earth, home to one-fifth of all humanity. The country looks modern and progressive—if you don't stray too far from the sites presented to tourists. If you do, you quickly find that human rights, democracy, free education, freedom of the press and certainly freedom of religion are all a facade—one that must be maintained at all costs. In China, saving face is of ultimate importance.

The Chinese constitution does in fact affirm religious tolerance, but those words mean something far different in that country than they do in Western nations. In practice, the government has placed a ban on all religious practices outside of officially recognized organizations. There are only two sanctioned Christian organizations—a Catholic Church without ties to Rome and the Three-Self Patriotic Protestant Church. Because the government cannot ignore the countless underground churches and the millions of people who worship in them, churches have been offered the opportunity to register with the government and receive a degree of legitimacy. Some have accepted this uneasy compromise, but millions of Chinese Christians flatly refuse. They maintain that to register would compromise their faith by giving ultimate authority to the atheistic state rather than to God.

No one knows how many practicing Christians there are in China; estimates run from forty million to over a hundred million. And the vast majority of these Christians choose to worship in secret. It is illegal in China for more than ten people to gather for any activity that is not officially authorized. It is illegal to talk about God to anyone under the age of eighteen, anytime or anywhere. It is illegal for anyone—even authorized pastors, except in their churches at regularly scheduled services— to influence another person toward religion. In house churches, Christians are doing these very things, so they exist under constant and often severe threat and persecution.

Yet the churches grow and grow.

While we were in Beijing, a worker in the underground church network told us, "If you come immediately, I can take three of you to visit a house church." She did not have to ask twice.

Close to the outskirts of the city, we got out of our taxi and started to walk. "Don't look back," our leader told us. When she felt sure that we were not being followed, we doubled back and entered a labyrinth of inside streets, courtyards and alleyways. We ducked under a chain, went past rows of parked bicycles and landed before a doorway that looked like all the other back doors. When we hesitated, our guide pushed the door open, glanced around anxiously and hustled us inside.

We were ushered through the kitchen, past the woman who owns the house. She never looked up. In the next room, six self-conscious preteen girls and a five-year-old boy had gathered for Sunday school.

"There usually are more young ones, but it is Chinese New Year and their families took them to holiday celebrations," a ponytailed young woman of twenty explained in perfectly understandable English. She was the Sunday school teacher, daughter of the homeowner. Should authorities burst in, she would say she was giving English lessons to the children. She didn't say how she would explain the Americans in the room.

This was a part of the labyrinth of alleyways that led us to the Chinese house church. [Photo - Rachel Johnston]

It was not surprising to see two women taking leading roles in this church. Three-quarters of the worshipers in Chinese house churches are women, as are half of their leaders.

The older woman came in with glasses of juice, which she set on a small wooden table in the middle of the room.

"That's where we do baptisms," the daughter said, gesturing to the table. "Under the board is a cement pool."

Every Sunday close to fifty people crowd into that one room for a four-hour church meeting. "On Christmas we had two hundred," the young woman said. We asked why the congregation did not divide into smaller groups. She replied, "Because no one else offers their house."

Many in the Chinese churches are new believers who have had very little opportunity to grow and mature in the faith. Most have limited access to the Bible, and even less to mentoring and instruction from mature Christians. This means they are easy prey for cults and teachers of false doctrine.

The girls sang a song for us—quietly, so the neighbors would not hear—then recited Scripture in Chinese. The little boy also said verses for us. When, with shy grins, the children demonstrated their English expertise by reciting John 3:16, we joined in and joyously proclaimed with them: "For God so loved the world that he gave his only begotten Son, that whosoever believeth in him shall not perish, but have everlasting life."

The daughter's uncle, who also lived in the house, kept opening the door and anxiously looking in at us. No wonder he was nervous. More than ten people were gathered, four were foreigners, and children were being taught about God. If any of his neighbors in that cramped housing enclosure were to turn him in, the house would be seized, he could be imprisoned and beaten, and a hefty fine could be imposed.

After about ten minutes we were ushered into the kitchen. Suddenly the door burst open and a man we had not seen before gestured wildly and ordered, "Get out!"

We did. As we hurried away, we prayed for those we left behind, and we thanked God for a freedom we take for granted—simply to attend church.

4

Greater Love Has No One
GONG MAI'S STORY

Gong Mai was only ten years old when she became a proud card-carrying member of the Communist party. Shortly afterward, when her grandmother said something about God, Gong Mai warned her sternly, "That is foolishness, Grandmother. If you say it again, I will have to report you to my teacher!" Her grandmother never did.

Gong Mai passed her exams easily and went to the university in Beijing. But when her sister took the exams the following year, she failed. Rather than deal with the humiliation, her sister went out into the woods and drank poison. Only her grandmother shed tears.

When Gong Mai graduated, she was awarded a coveted position with the government, and there she advanced quickly. By year's end she was settled into an office that looked down on Tiananmen Square—"the Gate of Heavenly Peace."

One June day in 1989 Gong Mai stood at her window watching a student protest that had been gaining momentum since April. The square was now crowded with thousands of students who some were saying intended to overthrow the government. That seemed preposterous, yet no one could deny that change was in the air. Communism was crumbling in the Soviet Union, and in the heart of China students were rallying for democracy, something that never would have happened a few years earlier when she was a student. Matters had become serious enough that martial law had been declared.

Chinese troops and tanks rolled toward the square, but where, Gong

Mai wondered, were they going to go? Hordes of people blocked their way. Suddenly, to her dismay, the troops began to shoot. People—even innocent bystanders—were falling everywhere. Gong Mai could not believe her eyes.

And then the most amazing thing happened. A young man stepped out in front of the advancing column of tanks and stood defiantly in front of them. The column advanced. The young man stood steady. The column slowed. The young man did not waver. The tanks stopped.

"I burst into tears," Gong Mai told us. "That man stopped those tanks with his own body."

Gong Mai grabbed her treasured Communist membership card and slammed it down on the table. She wanted nothing more to do with the party. She ran from the room, down the stairs and out into the street.

"From the age of ten to the age of twenty, I was a devoted member of the Communist Party," Gong Mai said. "Now I was nothing because now I saw the futility of it all."

Her first thought was to join her sister in death, but she lost her nerve. Instead she decided she would leave China, a country she saw as totally hopeless. Her plan was to take a six-month English course and then take a test for admission to an American university.

One day one of her professors, a young man from Australia, asked Gong Mai why she wanted to go to America to study when she had such a good job in China. He seemed genuinely interested, so she opened up and poured out her disillusionment.

"I know it is dangerous to be speaking what is in my heart," she said, "but I no longer care. Even if they kill me, what does it matter? I don't want to live one day longer with no hope."

"I know someone who can help you," the professor said.

"Who?" Gong Mai asked.

"His name is Jesus Christ," the professor answered. "It is written: 'Very rarely will anyone die for a righteous man, though for a good man someone might possibly dare to die. But God demonstrates his own love for us in this: While we were still sinners, Christ died for us.'"

Gong Mai went home, but she got no sleep that night. "A voice inside my head gave me no rest," she said. "I knew what the professor said was the truth, and I had to know more."

The next day she sought him out and asked, "How can I be a follower of Jesus?"

"Meet me in my office in one hour," he told her.

Gong Mai was met by the professor and three Christian Chinese women. First they talked, then they prayed together. They had no Bible to give her, but they showed her how to tune in to the Far East Broadcasting radio station, where she could hear Bible teaching. They also gave her cassette tapes.

Three weeks later, on the day of her big exam, Gong Mai awoke in excruciating pain. She was rushed to the hospital, where she endured a battery of tests. A serious infection that started in her ear had spread throughout her body; it kept her hospitalized for almost four months. She missed her test and along with it her opportunity to leave the country. And she never again saw the professor who had risked his life to point her to Jesus. But while she was in the hospital, she met a very kind young man who took tender care of her. After two months she dared to whisper to him the name of the One who had become her first love— "Jesus." The young man's eyes lit up. He too was a Christian!

Just before Gong Mai was released from the hospital, she and the young man were married. When she got out he took her to the underground house church where he worshiped. But because she was affiliated with the government, the Christians there feared and distrusted her. It was not unusual for Communists to infiltrate a house church and then turn all its members over to the authorities.

Desperate for income that would allow her husband to attend an underground seminary program, Gong Mai reluctantly went back to her old job. But it was not easy for a Christian to work there. "I was required to do my work, but my superiors would not allow me access to the documents I needed," she told us. "And then I was reprimanded for not doing a complete job. I could never advance, and I was constantly being scolded."

Gong Mai was threatened and humiliated daily. Finally she was forced to leave—but not until the very week her husband finished his seminary training.

Today Gong Mai and her husband lead an underground house church outside Beijing. Three months before we arrived, Gong Mai told us, there was a crackdown on house churches in their area, and the pastor and Sunday school teacher of a neighboring church were arrested. The pastor's farmhouse in which the church had been meeting was boarded up, and the two were taken to jail, where they were held for fifteen days.

"They were questioned day and night," Gong Mai said, "hardly allowed to sleep or eat. When they refused to disclose the names of other Christians, they were beaten and their families were threatened. Then they were thrown in jail, where the conditions are horrible. They didn't know what was happening to their families and the other Christians. But they stayed strong. They never gave away our names."

The pastor is out of jail and staying with friends, but he is a farmer, and without his land he has no way to earn a living. And because of the terrible conditions in prison, the Sunday school teacher is still very ill. That church has not yet found another place to meet.

Threats, intimidations and arrests are common experiences for leaders of Chinese house churches. And yet sometimes when they are arrested, so many Christian brothers and sisters visit them, singing hymns and praising God, that the jailers finally give up and set them free.

Because of the income from her government job, both Gong Mai and her husband have been able to receive seminary training, but their case is very unusual. Most house churches are led by farmers or whoever is willing to do the risky job.

"One of our big concerns is training new believers. It is so important that they are discipled well," Gong Mai told us. "Otherwise how can they stay away from false teaching? How can they share their faith well? And how can they stay strong under persecution?"

Kay said to Gong Mai, "You are living under constant threats, both for yourself and your family. What makes you keep on in the face of persecution?"

"I keep seeing that one young man who stood so bravely in Tiananmen Square and stopped the column of tanks," she said. "He was willing to face death for what he believed politically. How much more should I be willing to do whatever I am called to do to profess my Christian faith? The results are for eternity. Christ's love and peace are greater than persecution. They are even greater than death."

PRAYER POINT

Pray for the new believers in China, that they will be well grounded in their faith and able to stand firm for the Lord. Pray for wisdom and patience, and for endurance for mature Christians as they persevere and guide the young ones.

5

Beautiful Feet

ZHANG YUAN'S STORY

How beautiful on the mountains

are the feet of those who bring good news,

who proclaim peace,

who bring good tidings,

who proclaim salvation.

ISAIAH 52:7

Zhang Yuan and her husband had a partnership ministry, going house to house in the Chinese countryside to share the love of God in Christ. He encouraged and instructed the men, she the women and children. In their own village they led a thriving house church.

The closest registered church to their village was three hours' walk one way. In any case, few people trusted the registered church. There were many stories going around about sermons being tampered with and about a "gospel" that taught one to be a good Chinese citizen and made no mention of the Bible or of Jesus Christ. Thus Zhang Yuan and her husband, like many other Chinese Christians, feared that the compromises were too great. Even though it involved enormous risks, they preferred attending a church near home.

The Zhang church people did their best to avoid drawing attention. When they came for worship, they filed in quietly one or two at a time. And when they sang and praised God, they never raised their voices above a whisper. But good news gets around, and their numbers kept growing. Nearly every week there were new faces in the group. It was a good thing, yet everyone knew it could become a problem.

"You cannot be sure everyone is genuine in following Christ," they warned one another. "There could be informers among us." Still, everyone who visited was welcomed as a brother or sister.

Each week Zhang Yuan got the room ready for the service by moving their belongings out of the way while her husband spent time in prayer, preparing his heart before sharing from God's Word. Since they had no children, Yuan had time to visit the women of the church throughout the week. She always encouraged their faith and faithfulness to Christ. She understood that it was important that she never show fear of what the future might bring. In every way she wanted to communicate that God would always be with them and would be faithful to take care of them.

One night while Yuan was making a simple dinner of rice and vegetables with tea, she began to sense that hard times were coming for the little church. She paused to pray over the steaming stove: "Father, give us your wisdom and strength. Help each of us to remain faithful to you."

Darkness fell, but her husband did not come in from work. Zhang Yuan began to worry that he might be hurt and unable to get help. She put on her winter jacket and hurried toward the field to find him.

Yuan spent the entire night looking everywhere for her husband, even knocking on neighbors' doors. As the sun rose, she made one last walk through the field where he had worked every day for the past ten years. It was as though that field had opened up and swallowed him. With a heaviness she had never known, she walked back home and fell asleep.

Sometime later Zhang Yuan was awakened by a loud, crashing noise. Her house had been forced open by a group of men she had never seen. One picked up her prized blue pottery bowl, examined it, then smashed it to the floor. Yuan leapt from her bed and ran from man to man, her hands outstretched, trying to save her belongings. It was futile. Everything was being smashed, ripped, stomped, crushed. Finally, resigned, Zhang Yuan slipped to her knees and prayed silently while the men tossed books, Bibles, music sheets and papers into a heap in the center of her home. She suddenly realized that these men were from the Religious Bureau and her home was being investigated for unregistered church activity.

When the ransacking was completed, Zhang Yuan was pulled to her feet and roughly marched to an interrogation house. "Your husband has been sent to a labor camp for leading illegal meetings," she was told. "He confessed to everything. You might as well confess too. Your home no longer belongs to you. Since you are the wife of a criminal, all your property is forfeit."

Yuan endured an entire day of being yelled at, slapped and beaten. Someone even spat in her face. As demoralizing as it was, her thoughts kept returning to her husband. All she wanted was to know that he was all right and that she would be able to see him soon.

When the authorities were finally convinced that Zhang Yuan was too stubborn to give away the names of other unregistered church members, they tossed her out into the village street. She was only a woman. What harm could she do?

Yuan dusted herself off and began to walk toward home. But then it dawned on her: *I cannot go home! I'm homeless!*

Still, something drew her back to the house, to whatever remained of her peaceful life before she was taken into custody.

When she rounded a curve and saw her little homestead, Zhang Yuan's tears began to flow. Even in the dark, she could see that the windows and doors had been boarded shut. How she longed to go inside. She sank down against the front door and sobbed out her pain to God.

"Yu-Yu, don't stay here. Come to my house. I have some soup waiting for you. You can tell me all about what happened." Yuan was grateful to see the kind, familiar face of Mrs. Lee from church.

Weeks passed as Zhang Yuan awaited word from her husband. The

Lees were wonderful. They made her feel that she was an important part of the family, and they begged her never to leave them. Yuan took up her ministry to women again. Many marveled at her faith despite all that had happened to her. She was a courageous example. If her husband was suffering for Christ, she would honor him by being bold for her Savior as well.

Still, some believers were openly frightened. Was it wise to start meeting for worship again? If they did, would someone else have to suffer as Zhang Yuan and her husband had?

And then one quiet evening the authorities came to the Lee home asking for Zhang Yuan. They wanted her for further questioning. She went along, hoping she would learn some news of her husband. Instead she endured a repeat of what she called "the day of torment." She lost track of time. All she can recall is a whirl of yelling, pressure for names and finally a statement that she would be punished with a heavy fine, payable immediately.

"A fine?" she cried out in frustration. "Don't you see I have absolutely nothing to give you? You have taken everything I have—my home, my belongings, even my husband! I have nothing left!"

"That is not true," the officer in charge said with a smirk. "We can see that you are still wearing shoes. We want everything. Give us your shoes!"

Zhang Yuan stared at the officer in disbelief. Then she quietly complied, taking off her shoes and handing them over.

"Your work is done. You won't be going house to house anymore," he said triumphantly. Then he commanded the other officers, "Crush her feet!"

With their heavy boots the men stomped on Yuan's feet until they were horribly mangled. Then they left her to crawl back to the Lees' house.

The officer was right in that Zhang Yuan can no longer go house to house. But he was wrong about her work being done. Today she still "stands" as a faithful witness. Women and children come to her bedside to hear her tell the story of a God who loves them and who sent his own

Son to suffer and die for them.

Today her crushed feet are more beautiful than ever on the mountain of God.

Prayer Point

Pray for our sisters and brothers who endure persecution and torture for the sake of Christ. Pray that their courage will bear witness, even to their persecutors.

6

China Trainer

POLLY'S STORY

$\mathcal{B}$efore World War II, Polly's wealthy parents moved out of mainland China to the British-controlled island of Hong Kong, seeking a life of freedom for their family. They brought with them horrific stories of the suffering of the Chinese people. Polly grew up so affected by these stories that she never identified herself as Chinese. When asked her nationality, to this day she says, "I am a Hong Kong people—not a mainland China people."

Though they had lived a life of wealth in China, Polly's father lost his money through bad investments in Hong Kong. In dejection, he left the family and went to sea for three years. Polly's mother and aunts survived by sewing clothes for people.

When her father finally returned home, he took an office job in a school. During his travels he had learned to speak English, and this made him a valuable worker. The family was allowed to live on school property.

"There was a large tree there," Polly recalled. "One day it caught fire. Everyone insisted that they saw a god living inside that tree. My mother was worried for me, because I was a sickly child. So to protect me, she named me a Chinese name that sounds like 'Depend on that tree.'"

Polly's mother was miserable living with her abusive sisters-in-law. Then one day someone told her about the love of Jesus and invited her to come to church with her daughter. She found the church people to be loving, accepting and kind. Polly remembers playing in the back of the church when she was eight years old. "Sometimes I dozed off, sometimes I played, but I was always overhearing and learning." Polly, like her mother, accepted Jesus as Savior.

One night when she was a young adult, a visiting pastor preached an especially long sermon. "I forgot most of everything he said, but I'll never forget the last part," Polly said. "The pastor told us that one in two Americans is Christian, one in fifty Europeans is Christian, but only one in five hundred Chinese is a Christian."

One in five hundred? Polly thought. *Then what happens to those other 499? I have responsibility for 499 souls!*

Polly could not get those Chinese souls off her mind. But, she reasoned, if she were to go to China and tell them about Jesus, she would have to be ready to explain the gospel correctly, using the Bible, and to answer their questions. She would need to get training in a seminary. How could she do that? She was the oldest child in her family with two small brothers still in elementary school.

"Surely this is not what you want me to do," Polly told God. "I will go if you want me to, but surely you don't."

The same weekend a woman in the church told Polly that a young Christian man was interested in her. The two had grown up in the church together, and Polly liked the young man very much. But he had plans of his own, and going to China was definitely not included.

"Why would you bring this nice young man to me and then ask me to go to school and then to China?" Polly asked God. "I will do that if you want me to, but it doesn't make sense to me. I don't think it is really what you want me to do."

For a year and a half, Polly argued with God. "Finally," she said, "I stopped arguing and joined the seminary in Hong Kong. After that I began working in Hong Kong, sharing Christ in high schools and elementary schools. I also worked on publications for our ministry."

Polly's first trip into China was filled with unknowns. Her boss told her to be sure to take along lots of Kool-Aid. "I didn't know what Kool-

Aid was. I am a single lady with no children, so I never made it before. But I obeyed his request and packed plenty."

Her head was still filled with the horror stories from her childhood. She was told that a person would meet her once she arrived in the mainland. For her protection, she could not be told what kind of work she was to do, nor could she know where the meetings were to be held.

"When I arrived, a man met me and gave me a special signal," Polly said. "He hurried me into a car with dark windows, and we drove away."

The road grew increasingly bumpy. "I call that my 'lose weight car' because it pounded my body so much," Polly told us.

Her first night in China was cold and drizzly. Yet she was up at 2:30 the next morning, since at 3:00 they were to leave for a meeting. When they arrived, there were over two hundred people sitting in the cold rain, waiting for the service to begin. Many of them had walked long distances for the privilege of being there. Suddenly thunder rolled and a flash of lightning lit the sky.

"I begged the Lord to have mercy on those miserable people and stop the rain," Polly said, "but it just kept pouring down on them."

By 5:00 over seven hundred people were crowded into the unmarked church building. Polly was instructed to begin making Kool-Aid for the first Communion of the new believers who were to be baptized after the simple service.

"One man wrote down the name of every person who went into the baptismal to be baptized that morning," Polly said. "Our final count was 771."

When a man came forward in a beautiful silk suit and expensive leather shoes, everyone gasped. "By this time, after so many had been baptized, the baptistery was little more than a muddy pool. But that man didn't hesitate one second. For him, ruining his nicest clothes by baptism was an honor."

Shortly after noon, everyone who had made it through the rain had been baptized. Each person was given a small dumpling before starting the long walk home.

"I kept thinking that was not enough to give them," Polly said. "How I wished I had a Bible for each new believer. God so touched my heart for those dedicated people. I knew that moment that I wanted to spend the rest of my life helping them grow the church."

Only later did the ministry team learn that the police knew about the baptism and had planned to break up the meeting and conduct mass arrests. The officers had been discouraged by the heavy rains Polly had begged God to stop.

An elderly woman stumbled through deep, muddy furrows only to find an empty mud hole. She had arrived too late. Everyone was already gone except one man who was just leaving. "When will I ever have a chance to be baptized?" the distraught woman sobbed. "I came so far!"

Polly would be back many times for many women. She continues to travel throughout China as a mobile "seminary" for house church leaders. Depending on the courses that need to be taught, she stays at a clandestine site for five to ten days before she moves on to another church.

Polly has been arrested, threatened, interrogated and detained, yet she is always ready to go back. And she is not alone. Polly is representative of thousands of single Chinese women who believe that to know Christ is to serve him, no matter what the cost.

PRAYER POINT

Pray for perseverance for Polly and the other single Chinese women who labor for the Lord as mobile seminary teachers. Ask God to protect them from loneliness and discouragement and to keep them safe as they serve the house churches in China in this vital way.

MACAO

Population: 461,833

Religion: 50% Buddhist, 15% Christian,
                    35% other and none

Adult Literacy: Male 93%, Female 86%

Government: Special administrative region of
                    China

$\mathcal{I}$n 1997, when Hong Kong reverted to Chinese control, the entire Western world held its breath. What a prize for China. What a loss for the rest of the world.

In December 1999 Macao also reverted to China. Now it too is ruled as a special autonomous region under the "one country two systems" formula of government. However, there was not nearly so much fanfare about this change. Macao isn't the economic powerhouse Hong Kong is. But for the people who live on the island, it was a huge event.

In Asia, the former Portuguese island of Macao is known mainly for its glittering, neon-lit casinos, bars and massage parlors. In fact, a major part of its income is its proceeds from gambling. This has attracted the attention of Chinese gangsters, whose deadly battles over the potential fortunes in racketeering and extortion are a growing problem.

But there is another important "strip" in Macao. In 1993 the Macao Evangelical Church built a seven-story building to function both as the mother church for its ministry—which encompasses thirteen individual churches with a total of over 100,000 people—and as a training center for Christians in Macao and mainland China. Since then, teams of church leaders have come from China for training that is not available in their country.

Those who run the casinos have received assurances from the Chinese government that Macao's liberal climate will be protected.

How will the religious climate fare under the regime? Only time will tell.

7

From the Rooftops to the Mountains
MRS. CHEN'S STORY

A boat ride from Hong Kong to the peninsula of Macao—what an inviting idea! Our travel-weary team of women was ready for a refreshing experience.

"Look," our leader told us, "all I could get was first-class tickets. We are going to get a wonderful ride!"

The massive bargelike boat groaned away from the shoreline and cut its way through choppy water toward Macao. On the way over we compared notes about what we were learning from the women we had interviewed.

Mrs. Chen and her husband are the leaders of a large church in Macao. The day after their wedding in the 1960s, the Chens began to work with people who had been resettled from mainland China to Macao, and they have continued to minister for forty years.

A Portuguese colony since the sixteenth century, Macao offered unusual liberties for Chinese people for generations. Today, with its distinctive status as a special administrative region (SAR) of China, there is still a high degree of openness. From this platform the Chens have been able to reach out to many people with the love of God.

As a young couple, they began by addressing some of the most urgent needs of the resettled people in both Macao and Hong Kong. There is very little land on either island, so the only places available to refugees or "resettled people" were the rooftops of apartments and office buildings. Over the years the Chens and their coworkers invested their labors in building a network of schools, homes, churches and entire social systems on the rooftops of Hong Kong and Macao.

As their own family grew, the challenges of the growing ministry were great. "We had the schools to run and the staff to oversee," Mrs. Chen told us. "We pastored a church that was growing, and our vision was growing too. I had those challenges and I also had children to raise. I was often torn. The Lord helped us manage, but it was difficult."

The Chens eventually received a surprising amount of public recognition for their efforts on behalf of the poor. The government was grateful for their hard work and their creative solutions to what seemed to be insurmountable problems.

As the couple saw God bringing so many to himself in Hong Kong and Macao, they grew increasingly restless to extend their work into China. "The poor around us now had access to so much help," Mrs. Chen said, "but what about those deep in the mountains of mainland China? They were so isolated. They had no one to show them the love of God."

As the Chens worked with the government in Macao, God granted them unusual favor with officials who were not generally inclined to be helpful to Christians. Those officials, by God's grace, opened doors for them on the Chinese mainland. The couple trekked with Chinese officials into the mountains to find the most remote, impoverished Chinese villages. "What we saw broke our hearts," Mrs. Chen told us. "We would start with just one village, and when we saw success, we would try to do somewhere else what we had just done in that place."

The Chens' strategy is to "adopt" one village and bring community development in every one of its areas of need. With the exception of a few occasional outsiders, their development workers are Chinese. The Chens provide training and materials for simple clean water systems; "lend" goats to provide income and meet basic needs for families; develop animal husbandry training; build medical clinics, churches and schools for children; and conduct one-year intensive training for pastors and church leaders.

"We have seen so many villages transformed by God's love," Mrs. Chen said. "Someday you must come back wearing your toughest shoes. We will take you to a village we are working with and to another we want to bless."

As we listened to her, our thoughts went back to what we had heard from the leaders of the house churches. They had been very fearful of cooperating with the government. We couldn't help but remember all the stories of persecution and deception and betrayal by Chinese authorities.

"Why do you think your ministry is able to work freely with the officials while others cannot?" Michele asked. "We've been hearing so many stories about religious suppression in China. Help us understand."

"Anything you say about China is true!" our Chinese travel companion said. "This country is immense. In some regions the officials are extremely oppressive toward Christianity, in others there is more freedom."

Mrs. Chen simply said, "God has granted us favor with the officials."

As we boarded the boat to cross back to Hong Kong, we noticed that the wind had picked up considerably. The water, mildly choppy in the morning, was now tossing with a frightening ferocity. And this time we did not have those first-class seats that made the earlier ride so pleasant. For almost two hours the boat rose and plunged, rose and plunged, as we fought a miserable head wind. We groaned in misery.

How can the same trip be easy and pleasant at one time and very difficult and miserable at another? Just like the country we were visiting. "Anything you hear about China is true." For some it is viciously oppressive, while others enjoy significant freedom.

PRAYER POINT

Praise God for the way his work can prosper in the most inhospitable of places. Thank him that he allows the ordinary and the humble to confound the strong and the wise.

MONGOLIA

Population: 2,694,432

Religion: 96% Tibetan Buddhist Lamaist; 4% Muslim, shamanist and Christian

Adult Literacy: Male 98%, Female 97.5%

Government: Parliamentary

*T*wo great names from the pages of history are associated with Mongolia: Marco Polo and the great Mongolian ruler Kublai Khan. The two met in the thirteenth century as Marco Polo followed the Silk Road, the famous trade route. What he found was a land deep in the clutches of demonic powers of a shamanist religion. Kublai Khan boasted of his sorcerers and their great powers. Why, he said, they could make objects move on their own. His idols could speak, he insisted, and could tell the future.

No, Christianity was the better way, Marco Polo told Kublai Khan. Everyone in the civilized world knew it was a far superior religion.

Kublai Khan responded by presenting the great explorer with a challenge: send one hundred Christians to his kingdom. If they were able to prove the supreme power of Christ, he would become a Christian. He would also be baptized. Furthermore, he would see that his entire kingdom did the same.

The Western world never responded to Kublai Khan's challenge. No Christians went to Mongolia. Today under one one-hundredth of a percent of Mongols are Christians. More than 90 percent have never even heard of Jesus Christ.

For most of the twentieth century, Mongolia was controlled by the Soviet Union. Today the country is an emerging democracy. Mongolia's brand of democracy, however, is unique. At the time of this writing, laws and amendments are being considered that could severely restrict religious freedom in Mongolia. Already authorities are declaring that according to the constitution only the Buddhist and Islamic faiths may be propagated.

Christians around the world need to unite in prayer for Mongolia.

8

The Long Journey

YE-LING'S STORY

*P*ut some things in a box you can carry," Mrs. Chao told Ye-Ling. "You and Mrs. Wan and I are going on a long train trip to Shanghai."

Ye-Ling was getting used to traveling, now that she was working as an itinerant Bible teacher in Mongolia. But she had been walking from village to village to tell people the good news of Jesus Christ. She had never before ridden a train. And to Shanghai? She had heard about that wonderful city, but she was from a small village in northern China.

The train station was packed with more people than Ye-Ling had ever seen in her life. And when the train approached, she dropped her box and clapped her hands over her ears. The noise was nearly intolerable.

"Get on the train," Mrs. Chao told Ye-Ling when the train stopped. But she was too terrified to get into that loud monster that raced along such a slender track. Her companions had to do a good bit of coaxing to get her into the cattle car. There were no seats, so the three women settled themselves on a pile of straw.

"Hold your bag closely, Little Flower," Mrs. Wan told Ye-Ling. "If you fall asleep, you could awaken without your things."

"We will take turns sleeping and watching over each other," Mrs. Chao said. "In three days we will be in Shanghai."

By the time they arrived on the third day, the three women were tired, stiff and very thirsty. But Ye-Ling hardly noticed the discomfort. She had gotten used to the noise, and her mind was spinning. She had never before been to a city, and there was so much to see! All the roads were level and black, not at all like the rocky dirt roads at home. Bicycle bells rang constantly and car horns never stopped honking. And the buildings—they were much taller than any tree Ye-Ling had ever seen. Why, they must reach all the way up to the clouds!

Mrs. Chao led the others to a bus stop and paid the driver with a paper ticket. She said they were going to a hotel to meet visitors from the United States.

"They came to hear our stories and to pray for us and China," she told the others. "We must be sure they also pray for Mongolia."

When they got to the hotel, Ye-Ling followed the other women into a small golden closet, and the door closed behind them. To her dismay, the closet began to shake and move. It made her stomach feel strange and uncomfortable. Suddenly the door opened, and they all got out. She followed the others down a beautiful hallway until Mrs. Chao stopped and knocked on a door.

It was an amazing room: two beds, a desk, a television, a radio and its very own bathroom. Ye-Ling stood and stared with her mouth open until Mrs. Wan pulled her aside and whispered, "The visitors from the United States need these things, Little Sister. In America everyone has them."

The women took turns telling stories of what it is like to be itinerant Bible teachers in Mongolia. They talked of the people's belief in demons. They told of the problems for Christians there given that the traditions and history of Mongolia are seen as purely Buddhist, Islamic and shamanistic. They talked of their ministry as Chinese missionaries. And they spoke of the suffering of the few Mongolian Christians: "Many Christians don't have others they can worship with, and they are afraid of what will happen to them if they do meet together. If they arrange secret meetings, the Christians dare not sing out loud of their love for God. Someone might overhear them and accuse them of speaking against the government or of proselytizing."

Mrs. Chao leaned forward and said earnestly, "We came to see you because we want you to know there are Christians in Mongolia and we are working there to tell all Mongolia about Jesus. We want you to ask the Christians in America to pray for those Christians and to pray for us in our work."

The three women prepared to head back to the train station, where they would board the cattle car for their three-day journey back home.

"One day we will meet again," Ye-Ling said.

PRAYER POINT

Ask God to protect the team of Chinese women in Mongolia as they continue their outreach. Their leader was imprisoned in 2002 for holding Bible clubs for children; she was released later that year.

East Asia

PRAYER POINTS

- Pray for both the house churches and the registered churches of China. Though their number is growing, many do not have access to good Bible teaching. Without a solid foundation in the Bible, believers can be confused by false teaching and become easy prey for cults.

- Pray for more open churches. There are only four open Protestant churches in all of Beijing, a city of thirteen million people.

- In China today there are more Christians in prison because of religious activities than in any other nation in the world. Pray that the believers can stand strong in the face of severe persecution. Pray for God's peace for them as they suffer and, if it be his will, for their speedy and safe release.

- Pray for wisdom for Chinese pastors and Christians as they face difficult decisions concerning how best to meet the needs of worshipers: registering the churches or remaining underground. Pray for them as they face harassment and heavy fines and risk their personal liberty by preaching or even by worshiping with others.

- Pray for the training and strengthening of Mongolian Christians and for their protection from spiritual attack.

- Pray that more Christians in this region will have access to God's Word. The New Testament is only now being translated into a version of the Mongol language that is understood today.

- Pray that more local Christians will be raised up and trained to serve as pastors and teachers.

East Asia

ACTION POINTS

- One of the most vital ministries of Sisters In Service is the sending of seminary-trained Chinese women to clandestine sites to teach and instruct house church leaders so they will be better able to lead their people. Since 75 percent of new believers in house churches are women, women are needed to disciple them in the Scriptures. You can help by praying for a teacher and sponsoring their classes. Your Bible study or fellowship group could adopt a teacher who is teaching the Bible to others.

- Many of the things we enjoy and take for granted in our comfortable lives are the direct results of slave labor by inmates, some of them Christians, in Chinese labor camps. According to several sources, most of our Christmas lights are produced that way. Every time you see Christmas lights twinkling, pray for the Christians imprisoned in China.

- Create an advocacy team for China. Make it your mission to get informed about what is happening to women in China. Sacrifice and speak up for programs that are making a difference for them. Contact the Sisters In Service headquarters for a list of opportunities.

- Adopt a village in China. Take the village into your heart, your prayers and your everyday life. Tell people about your efforts to bless this village with the love of God. Your partnership in village projects will help generate such things as pig farms, a school, clean water systems and the discipling of local people. Ask others to join you in loving this village for Christ's sake.

PART 3

North Africa

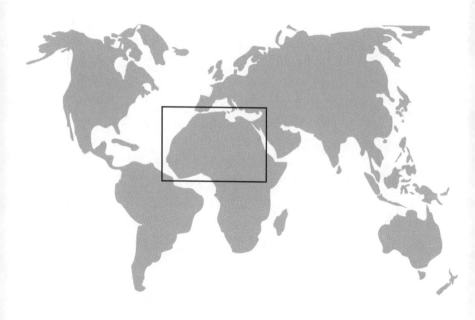

SENEGAL

Population: 10,589,571

Religion: 94% Muslim, 5% Christian,
1% indigenous beliefs

Adult Literacy: Male 51%, Female 28.9%

Government: Democracy

*A*s we headed out of Dakar, the capital of Senegal, the day was still relatively cool. We drove along a narrow paved road, dodging donkey carts and herds of goats, for an hour and a half before our driver made a sharp turn and headed onto an expansive plain that stretched out endlessly under a scorching sun. A large red monkey stared at us from the base of a giant baobab tree. It would be almost another hour of bumping through the sun-baked terrain along a faint dirt track before we glimpsed the sharpened-stick goat pens that let us know we were approaching a village. We were to meet with workers who were providing nutrition and health instruction to mothers with little ones in tow. Later they would be telling Bible stories to the village women and children.

"Give our women hope," a woman in Dakar had pleaded the night before.

I could not get those words out of my mind. Senegalese husbands make the decisions in the family. They hold the money and they have the power. As in many Muslim countries, a man can have up to four wives and many children. It is up to the wife to see that her own children have food to eat and, if possible, a bit of education. That is no small order when fetching drinking water means carrying heavy jars of it on their heads for four hours a day or more. Women get by as best they can.

When we arrived at the village, Oumi was there with a group of village women and children gathered around her. Twice a week she leaves the relative comfort of the city to share the gospel. "I became a Christian thanks to foreigners who came to Senegal to share God's Word. They left their comfortable lives and came here to see a Senegalese woman come to Christ. So I'm going to where other women are. I'm not going to wait for them to come to me."

A Senegalese woman brings her child to a health clinic. [Photo - Lisa Ringnalda]

Because of the profound poverty in the Senegalese countryside, men often leave the villages to find work in other countries, especially France. This means the women must struggle to survive alone.

"The thing that most draws them is prayer," Oumi told us. "Many have asked us to pray that their husbands will come back. Several have seen that prayer answered. Some ask for prayer that they will have children; one man came and prayed that his wife would have a child, and she did. With so much sickness here, the women often pray for healing. They take prayer very seriously and are moved by a God who will listen to women and answer their prayers. That is not the God of Islam. Muslim women believe God is too distant to ever be approached with a personal problem. Only a big marabou like Bamba, who is revered as a great Islamic imam in Senegal, can communicate with God—never a lowly woman." (A marabou is a leader of a mystical order of Islam unique to Senegal.)

Now, largely through the efforts of their courageous sisters, women in Senegal and across North Africa are learning about the true God of love and grace.

9

The Name of Jesus

SONGA'S STORY

From the time Songa's father arranged her marriage at fifteen, she knew the reason she was being added to her new husband's family. His first wife was worn out and needed help. With seven children to care for, a herd of sheep and goats to tend, a field of wheat and millet to work, and all the cooking and household chores to do, the first wife's days were far too full. And then there were the hours that had to be spent trudging back and forth in search of drinking water for the family.

"Don't worry," her mother told her. "Husbands always like their second wives best."

"Until they take a third wife," Songa said sullenly.

Actually Songa never noticed any preference from her husband, but she certainly felt animosity from the first wife. She kept Songa running from early morning to late at night. When Songa gave her husband first one son and then another, the first wife burned with jealousy.

On a trip to get water, Songa stopped to rest with some other village women, and there she heard stories about a God-man called Jesus the Christ who loves women and cares enough about them to listen to their prayers. Songa's baby son was sick with the same fever that had killed the first wife's third child. She untied the baby from her back and asked the Christian women to pray for him. They did, and to her amazement her baby got well.

From then on Songa made it a point to get up and leave early for water so she could spend time hearing the amazing stories about Jesus and his Father, the true God who cares about people, even women and children. The women discussed the stories they heard and what it would be like to worship a God who actually reached out and became involved in their lives. They prayed together and were amazed at how this Christian God heard and answered their prayers. The teacher told them the stories came from the Bible, but that did not mean much to any of them since none of the women could read.

Later, when they met at the well to fill their jars, the women in the group would whisper the Bible stories to each other until they knew them word for word.

When Songa's husband was away, his wives did not concern themselves with the regular Muslim prayers. But when he was at home, he insisted that they kneel behind him and his oldest sons and pray five times a day. For a time Songa continued to pray to Allah in Arabic as her husband instructed.

"But I knew Allah was not the God of prayer," she told us. "The Christian God was the God of prayer. Wasn't I blaspheming by praying to Allah? I could not continue to be unfaithful to the true God."

So Songa, bowing on her prayer rug behind her husband and his first wife's sons, began softly praying, "In the name of Jesus. In the name of Jesus." She said it in her native Serere language rather than in Arabic.

The oldest son heard Songa's prayer and told his mother. The next time they were called to pray, the first wife listened carefully to what Songa said. Sure enough, it was a prayer in Jesus' name. Immediately she reported it to her husband. He was furious.

"Don't you ever pray in Jesus' name again!" he ordered.

"I am sorry, Husband," Songa said, "but I can never pray to anyone but Jesus. He healed my son and he answered my prayers. I am a Christian, and I cannot believe in any other God. I will respect you, but I will be faithful to Jesus."

"You will obey me and pray to Allah or I will beat you and throw you out of my house!" he threatened. "And your children will stay here. They are Muslims and they always will be!"

The next day, at the time of the first prayer, Songa's husband situated his prayer rug where he could hear her prayers. Asking God for courage, she boldly said, "In the name of Jesus. In the name of Jesus."

Her furious husband beat her repeatedly with a stick. Then he demanded, "How will you pray?"

Songa answered, "In the name of Jesus, Husband."

"Get out!" he ordered. And he pushed her out the door.

The last Songa saw of her children was them crying in the doorway.

Songa is now remarried to a Christian husband and is the mother of three more children. She still goes to the village, but now she is one of the teachers who tells Bible stories to the women who stop by on their way to get water.

"The more I tell the stories to others," she told us, "the more precious they are to me."

We were quiet as we tried to comprehend the pain of having to choose between Jesus and our children. It was Songa who broke the silence: "God has given me so much. I am the only wife of a good husband. We worship God together. I have healthy children. I can raise my children to know the true God."

Yet when we asked Songa how we could pray for her, tears came to her eyes. "Every day I pray for my other children, that God will show them he is the true God. Will you pray for that too? Will you pray for my boys?"

We told her we would.

PRAYER POINT

Pray that God will draw Songa's boys to himself and will grant her the joy of seeing them serve the one true God. Pray for Christian mothers and fathers around the world, that they will remain faithful and strong as they seek heavenly guidance for their children.

10

Drawn by the Spirit
JUSTINE'S STORY

Justine was raised on the banks of the Gambia River, where her father, like the fathers of all her friends, grew peanuts in the sandy soil. But unlike all her friends, who were Muslim, her family was Catholic. They attended a tiny Catholic church and prayed to the saints just as they prayed to their ancestors on the altars at home. Her father had a Bible, and on holidays he read a few prescribed verses from it, but Justine was not allowed to touch it. To her it was a mystery book.

In 1997 she met a young woman who said she also was a Christian. When Justine mentioned her desire to read a Bible someday, her new friend said, "Come with me to a women's retreat this weekend. I think you will like it. They are going to have debates on biblical topics."

Justine had been taught to be extremely careful whom she trusted. She had already been careless in talking to a stranger about being a Christian. This could be a trap.

"I'll come, but only for a short time," Justine answered.

She enjoyed the discussions so much she ended up staying for the entire weekend. But when it was over the women told her, "Justine, debates are interesting, but you are not going to understand the Bible. All you can do is pray, and maybe God will help you figure out a little bit about it."

Frustrated, Justine went home and dug out a New Testament she had won in a contest at church years earlier. Remembering what the women had said, she knelt by her bed and prayed for a little bit of understanding. Then she read the first five chapters of the book of Matthew. The next day she read five more chapters, and the next and the next. Each day she would pray first, then read more chapters.

"I was absolutely amazed because it seemed that God was talking to me personally about my own life," Justine told us. "It made me uncomfortable, yet I couldn't stop reading."

She thought she should go to church, but she had no desire to pray to the statues there; they seemed cold and lifeless. And she certainly did not want to pray to the ancestors. "When I talked to them, I knew no one was listening."

When her parents saw that she was spending much time reading the Bible and not following their religion, they were upset with her. "Why are you doing this?" her father demanded. "If you had to change religions, it would be better for you to be a Muslim. That way you wouldn't risk bringing the anger of our ancestors down on us. Our ancestors are in this land. They see that you do not respect them."

It was the season of the harmattan, hot, dusty winds that blow off the Sahara. The next day when Justine's brother was tilling the peanuts, a sudden dust storm blew up and hit him in the face, leaving him blinded. His sight did not return for three days.

"It is the anger of the ancestors!" Justine's father cried in terror. "We must leave this place!" They left the peanut farm and moved from Gambia to Senegal, away from the vengeful eyes of the ancestors.

"I felt sorry about the problems I was causing," Justine said, "but I couldn't put the Bible down." By this time she was reading ten chapters a day and copying the verses that meant the most to her into a notebook so she could memorize them. Soon she had filled two notebooks with verses and memorized them all.

"I decided I should marry a Muslim man so I could show him what it is like to be a Christian," Justine told us. This frightened her parents terribly, but her mind was made up. She met the man and set the date.

Justine told us, "Not long before the marriage was to take place, I read 2 Corinthians 6:14: 'Do not be yoked together with unbelievers. For what do righteousness and wickedness have in common? Or what fellowship can light have with darkness?' I knew immediately it was God warning me that I was making a mistake. I broke off with the Muslim man the very next day."

Justine was not prepared for what happened next. The authorities came to her house to force her to go through with the marriage. Only then did she learn that by marrying a Muslim man she would be forced to convert to Islam. Rather than argue or struggle, Justine simply repeated the words of 2 Corinthians 6:14 over and over and over again. Finally, with no explanation, the authorities turned and walked out of the house. She never heard anything further from them or from the Muslim man. God's Word had delivered her.

Justine knew no other Christians in her village in Senegal. She had no one to instruct her, encourage her or walk alongside her. But God drew her to himself through his Word, and the Holy Spirit was her teacher and guide.

As Justine pored over the Scriptures, her family heaped ridicule and insults down on her. "You're insane!" her brother taunted. "We are going to have you put in a hospital for crazy people!"

Even her few friends deserted her. "It's dangerous to be around you," one told her. "You can believe in God, but you shouldn't talk about it. You are going to bring trouble."

Only her mother tried to reach out. "I don't know this God of yours," she told Justine. "I don't understand. But if you are determined to serve him, then do it. You are an adult."

Yet even her mother wavered when Justine's brother and sister told her, "If you get sick, Justine will desert you. She will say her Bible told her to leave you all alone. And when you die, she will forget you ever existed." Terrified and in tears, Justine's mother confronted her daughter with these accusations.

"Oh, no, Mother!" Justine said. "The Bible says I am to honor my father and mother. If I don't do that, how can I possibly honor my Father in heaven? If I don't come to you when you're sick or when you die, that will be proof that I'm not an obedient child of God. A good Christian would want to do these things and take care of her mother." Justine used verses from her father's old Bible to back up what she said.

"If your father's Bible says it, then it must be true," her mother said.

"Mother," Justine said, "you're the one who brought me into the world. But can you take me to heaven?"

"No," her mother answered, "I cannot do that."

"Oh, Mother, don't you see? That's why I believe in Jesus Christ!"

None of Justine's family has accepted Christ. Although they live in the same house, neither her brother nor her sister will speak to her. She is constantly bombarded with the superstitions and fears that come from ancestor worship within her family and from harassment from the Muslim society in which she lives. But God has blessed her with a job in a clinic with other Christian believers, and for this she is most thankful.

Justine is unwaveringly certain of what she believes, and she can back it up chapter and verse. And she is not ashamed of the gospel of Christ for, as she loves to quote, "it is the power of God for the salvation of everyone who believes" (Romans 1:16).

"Do you get discouraged with so much opposition on every side?" we asked.

Justine flashed her bright smile and shook her head. Then she quoted a Senegalese proverb: "The big pot takes a long time to boil out, but when it does, it boils lots of food to serve many people."

The fire has certainly been lit under the pot in Justine's corner of Senegal. Soon the time will come when we will rejoice together in the glorious results!

PRAYER POINT

Praise God for the saving power of his holy Word. Pray that Christians around the world will see the importance of hiding God's Word in their hearts. Pray for those who do not have access to the Bible, that God will provide a way for them to hear and learn Scripture.

ALGERIA

Population: 32,277,942

Religion: 99% Sunni Muslim, 1% Christian and Jewish

Literacy Rate: Male 73.9%, Female 49%

Government: Republic. Democratic elections in 1992 gave victory to an Islamic political party, but the army annulled the results. Fundamentalists are strongly working for the institution of shari'a law.

*T*he name Algeria brings to mind terrifying television news reports and pictures from newsmagazines, images of entire villages massacred during a civil war. People not considered "Islamic enough" lay in ditches with their throats slit. If we wanted to find a country that is inhospitable to the gospel, surely Algeria would qualify. Imagine our surprise to discover one of the truly great Christian success stories there!

In 1982 the government of Algeria forcibly removed all missionaries from the country. There were only four Algerian Christians, and they faced a choice: they could either give up and return to Islam or, through the power of God, strive to build the church of Jesus Christ in their hostile country. They chose the latter. They would do it by hosting churches in their homes. One woman, who to this day cannot risk being identified, stood especially strong. Against all opposition, and despite the fact that her own husband was Muslim, she continued to draw people in until her home church grew astoundingly large. She is known today as the mother of the church in Algeria.

A number of the Algerian converts emigrated to Paris, but they did not lose their love and concern for fellow Algerians. Primarily through their efforts, a Christian radio ministry from Paris into Algeria was begun, and it has been hugely successful. Where twenty years ago there were just four Christians, there are now an estimated forty thousand.

Ten thousand-fold in twenty years. Now that's a success story.

11

"Dear Madame . . ."

TANINA'S STORY

*T*anina was a poor Muslim girl who lived with her parents and brothers in the mountains of Algeria. Like her mother and most of the other women and girls in her area, she could neither read nor write. What use would she have for such skills? She would do nothing but stay at home and work. On the rare occasions when she ventured out, she covered herself from head to foot and was accompanied by her father. That was how it would be until her father found a husband for her; then she would go out only when accompanied by him.

The one joy Tanina had to relieve the monotony of her days was a radio. She listened to all kinds of music—soft, sad songs and loud tribal dances. She tuned in to stations where men told stories and read poems. And when her father accompanied her mother to the market and her brothers were at school, she listened to a strange and exciting station that told about the prophet Jesus and his Father, God.

All her life Tanina had heard that there was only one God and Allah was his name. He was referred to as "the merciful and compassionate," but he never seemed that way to her. To her, Allah seemed far off and impersonal, and especially lacking in compassion toward women.

But the God she heard about on the radio was different. To show how truly merciful and compassionate he was, he sent his Son to earth to lead mortals to heaven. Could this be true? Tanina had to know more.

One day when her oldest brother came home from school, Tanina went to him in secret and presented him with a plateful of his favorite sweets. "I made these just for you," she said. "If you will teach me to read and write, I will make treats for you every day."

"You? Read and write? Why would you want to learn that?"

Her heart pounded. If he should discover the truth . . . if he should tell her father she was listening to an infidel program on the radio . . .

"Because it might help me find a good husband," she lied.

To her relief, her brother was too busy enjoying the sweets to ask any more questions. After that he worked with her every evening, teaching her to read and write the Berber language. Each day Tanina hurried through her chores and rushed to prepare a special treat for her brother, then settled down to study the lesson he had given her. Even her brother was amazed at how quickly she learned. "It's only because you are such a good teacher," she told him.

As soon as she could manage it, she composed a simple letter to the radio station:

> I listen to you on Radio Monte Carlo. I like the songs you play and I am very much touched by your message of Jesus. But I must know, how can God have a son who was a man? Also, can you tell me more about the cross?
>
> From Tanina

The next morning, so nervous she could hardly speak, she approached her brother with downcast eyes. "Brother," she said, "today I am making an extra-special treat for you."

"Oh?" he asked. "What do you want now?"

"I wrote a letter to a radio station I hear. I want you to post it for me— and, please, to tell no one."

He stared at her quizzically. But he took the letter and tucked it into his coat.

There was one thing Tanina could not get out of her mind. It was what she had heard about the cross Jesus' enemies had made. They had nailed him onto it, and then they had hung him there to die. It seemed incredible that God's Son could actually be killed. But then she heard that Jesus was buried and that he came back to life again. People actually saw him walking around after he had been dead. Not even the great Prophet Muhammad had come back to life after he died! Tanina decided there must have been magic in that cross.

The next time she was at home alone, she took out a piece of paper and carefully drew a picture of what she thought a cross looked like—a large X. Then she hung it on the wall near where she slept.

That evening her mother saw the picture. "What is that, Tanina?" she asked.

"Just a picture of something I heard about on the radio."

"Oh," her mother said with a shrug.

One day an important man from the mosque came to talk with Tanina's father and saw the picture. "What is that on the wall?" he asked suspiciously.

"Just something foolish my daughter made," her father said. "It's nothing of any importance."

The man said no more, but he continued to look at it and scowl.

When Tanina's letter arrived at the radio station in Paris, it was passed on to Rebecca, an Algerian Berber who immigrated to France when she was twelve. Immediately Rebecca responded, doing her best to answer the girl's questions.

When a letter arrived for Tanina from Paris, her family was stunned. Her father, mother and brothers all gathered around to see who it could possibly be from. Tanina opened it and, to their amazement, began to read it aloud.

When Tanina's mother discovered the letter was in response to one her daughter had written, she exclaimed, "My sons have gone to school, and they have never written to a radio station. No one I know has ever written to a radio station. Yet my daughter—a girl!—learned to read and write so she could write to a radio station!"

But no one seemed to understand what the letter was really about.

In the months to come, Tanina wrote longer and longer letters, each one filled with more questions. Rebecca did her best to answer in terms the girl could understand. She longed to put Tanina in touch with a local Christian woman, but as far as anyone knew, there was no one in the area.

Tanina lives in an isolated mountain region. In any case, where believers can be found in Algeria, they are usually new Christians. Few have much experience, training or ability to teach others. There are not nearly enough pastors for the churches that are springing up around the country. And because culture mandates that women and men cannot be taught together, even where there are pastors the women are left out of the teaching.

So burdened is Rebecca for her people that she saves money all year long to enable her to spend a month in Algeria working with women who are eager to know about Jesus—women like Tanina. Thus it was that six months after Tanina had entrusted that first letter to her brother, Rebecca knocked at her door.

As Rebecca talked with the girl and her mother, it became clear that Tanina's idea of Christianity, based on the little interrupted snatches she heard on the radio, was terribly skewed. Tanina pointed out her picture of the sideways cross and told Rebecca, "I worship it every morning and every night."

"Oh, no!" Rebecca told her. "Don't worship a picture. Only worship Jesus Christ. When you worship him, you are worshiping God, because Jesus and God are one and the same."

Tanina's mother told Rebecca about the man from the mosque and his suspiciousness about the picture.

"Take it down," Rebecca warned. "You are running an unnecessary risk by having it on the wall."

Tanina was hesitant, for she believed it had magical powers. "That cross brought you to me," she insisted.

"No," Rebecca told her. "God saw your heart, and he brought me."

The three women talked all day. During Rebecca's month in Algeria, she came back several times and was able to study the Bible with Tanina and her mother. Before she returned to Paris, Rebecca prayed with them that God would continue to teach them through the radio. She encouraged Tanina to keep on writing letters and asking questions.

The next year Tanina's father made marriage arrangements, and his daughter was married to a Muslim man twenty-five years her senior who already had one wife and several children in Paris. He lives there with them six months of the year and in his home in Algeria the other six months. When her husband is in Algeria, Tanina listens to her radio in secret. But when he is in Paris, a small group of women meets regularly in her house and listens to the radio with her. Her mother is one of them. Tanina reads the Bible to the women and teaches them the things Rebecca taught her about the God they now know and love who truly is "the merciful and compassionate."

PRAYER POINT

Pray for Rebecca and women like her who are willing to sacrifice much in order to instruct new believers. Pray for the new converts, that they will have the teaching and encouragement they need and that they will mature to become mentors to others.

MOROCCO

Population: 31,167,783

Religion: 98.7% Muslim, 1.1 % Christian, 0.2% Jewish

Literacy Rate: Male 56.6%, Female 31%

Government: Constitutional monarchy

*C*asablanca has a great bazaar, we were told, a really interesting place to shop. That was good, because it looked as if we were in Morocco for two days with no one to interview. All our efforts to communicate with our contact thus far had met with silence.

Morocco is a hostile environment for Christians. According to local Christians, not only does anyone who becomes a Christian risk severe charges of treachery, but anyone who so much as has "illegal contact with foreigners" can face dire consequences.

Yet we were irresistibly drawn to this country that has a rich Christian history; Morocco is, after all, the land of St. Augustine, who lived here during the fifth century. The church does exist in Morocco today, but only with great difficulty. It is estimated that there are some five hundred believers in about twenty groups. Bibles are extremely hard to come by. Yet things seem to be changing. The late King Hassan II had bragged that he was a direct descendant of the prophet Muhammad. But when his son King Mohammed VI succeeded him to the throne in 1999, Mohammed instituted liberalizing changes that Moroccan believers are watching with cautious and prayerful optimism and Islamists are actively opposing.

When we got to our hotel room, there was a telephone call from our contact. We would be able to meet with a woman sometime the next day. Where? Not in her house; that would be too closely watched. Not in a hotel; any coming and going would be noticed and would be sure to raise suspicion. He would pick us up and think of a place. Pictures? Oh no, not even from behind! And no tape recorder.

"Enjoy the bazaar," he said. "I'll contact you sometime tomorrow."

12

Put Your Hope in God
MEHDI'S STORY

Mehdi's husband drove us to an empty back office and bustled us inside. While we talked he paced nervously outside, then busied himself watering a few scraggly plants that grew against the building, then paced some more.

Mehdi seemed to be quite young, although it was difficult to tell. A scarf hid most of her face. "In case the authorities stop you," she explained apologetically. "It's important that you not be able to identify me."

She was a rare Moroccan, raised in a Christian home. "My family came to know Christ in 1972, and we have suffered for it ever since," Mehdi told us. "It is very hard to be a Christian in Morocco."

In the old part of the city where Mehdi grew up, everyone knew everyone else's business. Hers was the only Christian family, although the neighbors called them Jews. "In Morocco Christians and Jews are considered the same," she told us. "We're all infidels." In the mosques, people were warned against her family. Their name was even published in the newspaper.

School was especially difficult. The teachers despised Mehdi for defending her religion, and the other children mocked and ridiculed her mercilessly. Even the shopkeepers felt they had a right to cheat the family. When the abuse got too much to bear, Mehdi's family moved to another neighborhood.

"We are Christians inside our family," the mother told the children, "but outside you must not talk about it. It is too dangerous for you."

But even though they did not talk, people knew there was a Christian family in the neighborhood, and some figured out which family it was. "The only reason we were tolerated was that my mother was so good," Mehdi told us. "She helped everyone. Mama was kind and loving even to people who were very unkind to us. They couldn't help but respect her. The neighbor women would come to our house and say to my mother, 'You are a good woman. You only need to be a Muslim. Moroccans are supposed to be Muslim!'"

Although Morocco's constitution provides for freedom of worship, Islam is the official religion of the land and "proselytizing" is strictly prohibited. Anyone who attempts to "shake the faith" of a Muslim can be imprisoned and hit with a hefty fine. Mehdi's parents and grandparents were arrested, jailed and fined on numerous occasions.

"The authorities try to get you to give them the names of other Christians and then to sign a paper renouncing Christianity," Mehdi said. "If you do, they will usually let you off with just a fine. But my parents and grandparents wouldn't give names and they wouldn't sign the paper. So they spent two weeks in jail, and when they got out, they continued to be harassed."

Mehdi and her husband live on the other side of the city, where there are apartment buildings and people do not know their neighbors. They are much more careful. "We don't talk about our faith with our neighbors at all," she said. "None of them know we are Christians. It's important to stay quiet because the church meets in our house. Our neighbors pay little attention to the people who gather on Sundays, and we do all we can to keep it that way."

Although the law states they have a right to choose their religion, they do not have the right to have more than five people meeting together, nor can they legally host any type of religious activity in their house—especially a church.

"Every time we meet, we expect to be turned in," Mehdi said quietly. "If there is a knock at the door, we hurry to hide anything that could mark us as having a Christian meeting." That includes the one precious Bible to which the group has access.

Yet the church grows—slowly and cautiously, but it grows. Especially in women converts.

"The Qur'an teaches us to fear God," Mehdi explains. "We are told that everything in the Qur'an is from God. It is God who wants men to have four wives. A woman has to accept all the bad things done to her because it is in the Qur'an, so it is from God. Imagine coming from this background, then finding that another God exists, a true God who treats us in a different way. You cannot imagine how precious the love of God is to an Arab woman."

No, we told her. We cannot imagine. Tell us.

"In the Arab world the woman has no value at all, not a bit. But in Christianity women do have value. In Christianity we can express ourselves. We can talk and share an idea. Our Christian husbands have only one wife. Muslim women feel they alone are not enough for a man. I do not think you can understand it, but knowing God finally gives women value."

In Morocco, as in much of the Arab world, it is a great deal more difficult for women who come to Christ than for men. A woman believer has two choices: live as a secret Christian, alone and isolated, or tell her husband about her faith, knowing he will divorce her and throw her out of the house alone and destitute.

In Mehdi's small church there are several women who have been thrown out by their husbands. Because they are Christians, their families too have disowned them. They have no job skills, and they can barely read or write. The church has tried its best to support them, but the people are just too poor. To everyone's horror, one of the women starved to death. They found her when they came to church one Sunday morning.

In a voice barely audible, Mehdi said, "We finally agreed that without work they have to do whatever they have to do. Christian ladies have to . . . they have to . . . prostitute themselves." Choked with tears, she continued, "They can't help themselves. Their families do not accept them. The church can't feed them. To find a job in Morocco is not easy if you are a woman without qualifications. What can we do? Tell me, what can we do?"

We sat in silence and wept. We had no answers.

Mehdi's little church is doing something. They started a fund so they can provide one woman at a time with a loan to start a small business that will enable her to support herself. They already raised enough money for the first woman. She makes embroidery that she sells at a stand in the bazaar. It has been profitable enough to support her and also to repay a portion of her original loan. With extra contributions, there is enough in the church's fund to launch the next business for a talented woman who is painting Moroccan designs on magnets to sell to tourists.

Mehdi reached across the table and touched our hands.

In Morocco, women are able to set up small businesses in bazaars such as this one.
[Photo - Lisa Ringnalda]

"It is so important that people know about us," she said. "It is important that they care. Please, please pray for us."

We squeezed her hand and promised with all our hearts that we would—that we *all* would.

PRAYER POINT

Pray for women who are new converts from Islam as they struggle to establish a new life for themselves. Pray for the churches as they seek ways to help these women become self-supporting and become grounded in their faith.

TUNISIA

Population: 9,815,644

Religion: 98% Muslim, 1% Christian, 1% Jewish and other

Literacy Rate: Male 78.6%, Female 54.6%

Government: Republic with a strong presidential government and a virtual single-party state

*D*owntown Tunis could just as well be downtown London or Paris or New York City. Tunisia is one of the most progressive and open societies in the Arab world. Women there have many more rights than in most Arab countries. For example, men are allowed to have only one wife. Women are not at the complete mercy of their husband, and if the wife leaves, she has a chance to keep her children and even her house.

Yet with all the social progress, it is still not safe to be a Christian. The church must meet in secret, and should there be a knock at the door, worshipers must scramble to hide all evidence of a Christian gathering. Believers who become too visible face the loss of their job, persecution from the police and imprisonment.

Still, the church of Jesus Christ is growing in Tunisia. Three years ago there were just twenty known Christians in the entire country; today there are four hundred. "It's because the world joined together and prayed for us in 1999," one believer told us.

One evening we were sitting in a splashy outdoor restaurant with our host family, eating roasted chicken and french fries and shouting to make ourselves heard over the blaring rock music, when a young Tunisian woman in tight pants and a sequined top came over to chat with us. "We Tunisians are like you Americans," she said. "We just want to be rich and happy!"

Earlier that day I had had a conversation with a very different Tunisian, a passionate young believer. "You are standing on sacred ground," he told me, his voice overcome with emotion and eyes filled with tears. "This is the land of Christian martyrs and saints. It was here that people courageously went to their deaths, sawed to pieces and thrown to wild animals, all for their faith in Jesus Christ. So soaked was this ground in their blood that to this day its traces can be found in the soil."

For several moments I stood in silence, overwhelmed by the thought.

"Until the Muslim hordes came and wiped out the church?" I asked.

"That's what people think," he said. "But the truth is, by the time the Arabs arrived the church was nothing but an empty shell. The Christians had already destroyed it by fighting among themselves. In North Africa we have seen the disaster that comes from fierce divisions within the church. And we Tunisian Christians have made a vow: By God's grace, that will never happen to us again! In Christ's name we *will be* united."

When I asked how we could pray for the church of Tunisia, he said, "You want to pray for us? Then pray for yourselves. Pray for the church of America. Like many other Christians around the world whose lives are hanging in the balance, we depend greatly on you. And we are terribly afraid that arguments and splits are splintering and weakening you. Please, please—pray for the unity of American believers. That's what we pray."

That's also what Jesus prayed to the Father: "May they be brought to complete unity to let the world know that you sent me and have loved them even as you have loved me" (John 17:23).

Christians of the West: Do we just want to be rich and happy, as the young Tunisian woman said? Or can we learn from the Christians of Tunisia and dedicate ourselves to praying for the unity of believers?

13

A Lamp to My Feet and a Light to My Path

TAIZA'S STORY

*O*ur window in the house where we were staying in Tunis looked out on an ancient narrow street, worn away by a thousand years of foot traffic. One day at that window we were watching children playing in the sunshine when we saw two strangers approach and knock at the door.

"Cover up the books!" came an urgent whisper. "And your Bibles! Be sure they're hidden. Is there anything else that would give us away? Take the blankets on the bench by the stairs and cover everything up. Close the doors to your room and stay inside. Hurry now! Hurry!"

That was how it was whenever anyone stopped by who was not known to be safe. That is how Christians live in Tunisia, especially those who dare to host a church in their home.

Staying in our room with the door closed, waiting quietly for whoever had stopped by to leave, we heard a knock. We did not know whether to answer. Then came another knock. As we hesitated, the door was pushed open a crack.

"I'm a Christian," came a whisper in tentative English. "Can I tell you my story?"

We threw the door open wide. That was how we first met Taiza.

Taiza's Syrian father and Tunisian mother are both Muslims. "Twelve years ago, when I was studying history at the university, I got very curious about why Christianity disappeared from Tunisia when

Islam came," she said. "So for the first time in my life I began studying the Qur'an. But instead of finding the answer I was looking for, I found some very bad things, especially about Christians. I decided there was only one thing to do—look at the Bible and see what it had to say."

In her parents' attic Taiza found a copy of the Bible in Arabic. She opened it to Genesis 1:1 and started reading. She also continued to study independently about the persecution of the early Christians.

For a bright, ambitious young woman, Tunis was a good city in which to live. Taiza was able to establish a small bookstore and eventually to secure a permit to import books from France. It was a perfect business for someone who loved books and enjoyed learning and exploring new things.

In 1998 a woman came into Taiza's bookstore and cautiously asked for a particular book. Taiza recognized the title immediately, for it was a book she had read in her study of the persecution of Christians. Taiza's response was also cautious, but her curiosity about Christianity came through. Before the woman left a long while later, Taiza asked her, "How can I become a Christian?"

Over the next few months, the two met regularly in the back of the store to study the Bible together. Finally Taiza's new friend took her to a small church that met in a house across town.

"It's hard to bring a new person into a church," Taiza explained. "The authorities are always trying to infiltrate. Usually we can tell when someone is a plant. But last year a man who had been worshiping with us for an entire year turned out to be with the police. He had fooled us all. He turned us in, and we were all arrested."

For ten or twelve hours each of the church members was subjected to grueling questioning. They were threatened, harassed and pressured to give the names of other Christians and the locations of Christian activities.

"They kept asking me how I had become a believer in Jesus Christ and who had told me about Christianity. It made them very angry that I wouldn't tell them or give them names."

In the end not a single person in the church gave names, and everyone was finally released. But it was months before the group dared meet again, and of course they had to find a different location. "We started meeting on Friday afternoons like the Muslims do," Taiza said. "That is safer than meeting on Sundays."

There are very few Bibles and very little Christian literature available in Tunisia. "It's so hard for new believers to grow when they don't have access to the Bible," Taiza said. "If they can have God's Word, and also other books and literature, it is such a wonderful help to them."

"It's impossible," she was told when she asked about it. "There aren't any men who can bring that kind of material in—especially not Bibles. It just can't be done!"

"But I am doing it," she told us. "I am securing Bibles for the church and also other materials that will help new Christians to grow."

"How?" Michele asked her.

"By the grace of God," she answered.

It was several minutes before our minds began to register what this young woman, this four-year-old Christian, this wife and mother of two toddlers, was risking.

"Taiza," Kay asked, "if they should realize—if they catch you with those Bibles—Taiza, what would they do to you?"

A smile crossed her face. "I refuse to worry about it," she answered, "because my job is so very, very important. I am a Christian today because I got hold of a Bible twelve years ago. Do you know what a woman once told me? She said, 'I'm scared to read the Bible, because if I read it, in the end I may believe in it.' She was right. She read it, and she believed. That's why I have to get Bibles into this country. I have to do it even if it costs me my life."

We watched out the window as Taiza walked down the street with her husband and little children. Her smile never faded.

PRAYER POINT

Pray that Bibles will be readily available in Tunisia and in other countries around the world hungry for the Scriptures. Pray for those who risk so much to make them so.

SUDAN

Population: 37,090,298

Religion: 70% Sunni Muslim (in the north), 25% indigenous religions, 5% Christian (mostly in the south and Khartoum)

Literacy Rate: Male 57.7%, Female 34.6%

Government: Authoritarian regime. Current government is an alliance between the National Congress Party (NCP)—a front for the National Islamic Front (NIF), a fundamentalist Islamic political organization—and the military.

*W*ords like *hard* and *inhospitable* are inadequate to describe a country like Sudan. Christians suffer horrors in this war-torn country. For seventeen years civil war has raged in Sudan, pitting north against south, Arab against African, Muslim against Christian. An estimated two million people have died from war and related famine, and about four and a half million have become refugees.

Overt attempts to eliminate Christians from the country have included bombing Sunday church services and destroying hospitals and schools. Islamic troops attack unarmed Christian villages, murder the men, burn the buildings to the ground and carry off the children and women as slaves.

Refugee camps are horrific beyond description. Food is withheld from Christians who refuse to renounce their faith and embrace Islam. Women are raped, and both men and women are beaten and tortured.

The brutal acts are part of the National Islamic Front's declared jihad—holy war—on the south. Human rights observers insist that the NIF violates almost every provision of the Universal Declaration of Human Rights. It is believed that more people have died in Sudan than in Bosnia, Chechnya, Kosovo, Rwanda and Somalia combined. So why is there no great public outcry, no demand for justice?

Good question! The West has largely ignored the situation.

We have all heard the saying "All that is necessary for evil to triumph is for good men to do nothing." In Sudan the horror will not end until good people rise up and take a firm stand against what is happening to our Christian sisters and brothers in the south. And there is not a day to spare.

14

Mourning into Dancing
ANNA LIDU'S STORY

*L*ife has never been easy for Anna Lidu. Even though she was a bright child, at the head of her class in math and science, the civil war in her country made it difficult for her to get through school. Still, she completed her education to the highest level and became a medical doctor.

Setting up her practice was not easy either. That is because she is a Christian, and the National Islamic Front declared jihad on the Christians back in 1983. The most stable place in war-torn Sudan was the capital city of Khartoum, so that was where she settled. But as she looked at the physical suffering and despair around her, Dr. Lidu knew she could not work for money alone. So, using her medical practice as a platform, she set up the first indigenous women's ministry in Sudan and reached out to the "displaced persons camp" crowded with refugees.

None of the difficulties of her life had prepared her for what she would witness in this camp.

"We are overwhelmed," Dr. Lidu told us. "There are so many horrors, so many physical needs, so much injury, such terrible malnutrition. Even the water is contaminated. Diseases like meningitis are rampant. We do all we can, but sometimes I get so discouraged."

Dr. Lidu told of treating a woman who had been found on the road unconscious, with her breasts cut off. The villagers said that government forces were capturing women and asking them whether they were Christian or Muslim. If they answered "Muslim," they let them go. But if the response was "Christian," the women were raped, mutilated and eft to die where others could see them as a warning.

"This woman was supposed to be an example to others who would dare to remain Christians," Dr. Lidu said. "But I wish they could have heard her as she was recovering. She spent her time praising the name of Jesus!"

The refugees in the camp are Christians who have refused to renounce their faith. Many have witnessed things too horrible to imagine. Believers have been lined up and shot in the head with three-inch nails. They have been run over by Soviet-made tanks. They have been executed at point-blank range.

Now forced starvation is one of the Khartoum regime's primary means of persecution. When government forces attack a Christian village, they kill everyone they can, then they burn everything to the ground—houses, stored grain, crops in the field. Survivors who manage to escape the killing are left with no means of survival. There is no food, no water buckets, no tools, not even a bush for shelter from the scorching 115-degree heat. Stragglers do their best to survive in the arid wilderness on tree leaves and roots and stagnant, dysentery-infested water. A fortunate few stumble into refugee camps.

"All a family has to do is change their name to Muhammad or Ramadan," one puzzled government official has commented. "Why don't they do it? Just convert to Islam and walk the two days back to the government of Sudan."

That is the goal: convert the Christians and be done with them. Only it is not working. No matter what the regime does, the Christians just will not go away.

Always families in the camps talk with dread and fear of the Muslims who carry off their women and girls to sell them into slavery. This is another tool the NIF uses against Christians. They capture them and take them by train to slave markets in the north.

On top of the persecution, there are social ills that cause Dr. Lidu great despair. "We must also contend with the horrendous practice of genital mutilation and its complications," she said, shaking her head sadly. She described how girls are gouged and stitched at puberty in an attempt to ensure moral purity and secure a good dowry. A quarter of all the girls who undergo this barbarous procedure die—some from shock, some from infection. Those who survive have lifelong, sometimes debilitating problems.

"How do you do it?" Michele asked. "Isn't it just too much to see your people suffer so terribly?"

"Even when we can heal the injuries and the illnesses," Dr. Lidu said, "there is such poverty of the soul. I don't think you can imagine. There is such a lack of hope. People literally die because they have no hope."

Yet it is precisely because of their hope that every one of these people is here. It is because, despite all, they would not renounce their Lord and Savior. That hope may flicker, but it is there.

Dr. Lidu agreed. "What we do is revive the hope they already have," she said.

The team began holding tent meetings. They drew people in with their singing. The larger the crowd grew, the louder and more joyful the singing. Then there was an encouraging gospel message, followed by testimonies, then prayer.

"Our people love to sing and dance," Dr. Lidu said. "Before the war, it was a wonderful part of our worship. To bring it back revives their spirits, turning their mourning into dancing. Even the most persecuted, the most destitute people can have the joy and hope of Jesus Christ."

> The LORD . . . has sent me to bind up the brokenhearted,
>   to proclaim freedom for the captives
>   and release from darkness for the prisoners,
> to proclaim the year of the LORD's favor
>   and the day of vengeance of our God,
> to comfort all who mourn,
>   and provide for those who grieve in Zion—

to bestow on them a crown of beauty
  instead of ashes,
the oil of gladness
  instead of mourning,
and a garment of praise
  instead of a spirit of despair. (Isaiah 61:1-3)

PRAYER POINT

Pray that God will grant the Sudanese Christians an acute awareness of their great hope in Jesus in spite of their profound suffering. Pray for strength and wisdom for Dr. Lidu as she ministers to these courageous people.

North Africa
PRAYER POINTS

- Pray for good water for the villages of North Africa. Long treks in the oppressive heat to collect water are more than the women's under-nourished bodies can bear.

- Pray that the Christian city women in Dakar will become involved with women from the villages, make friends with them and teach the Bible in ways they can understand.

- Pray that women who have been reached for Christ will have the courage and resolve to leave their comfort zone and reach out to other women.

- Pray for the resistant, hard-to-reach tribes and peoples of North Africa.

- Pray for the people of Mauritania and Libya, the hardest, most oppressive countries in the area.

- Pray that God will raise up more pastors to lead the churches that are growing throughout Algeria. Pray for growth, maturity and wisdom for them as they mentor the new believers.

- Pray for women to teach and disciple the new women believers. In these countries, culture dictates that men do not work with women, so many Christian women are left with no one to guide and shepherd them.

- Pray that African Christians will have access to God's Word.

- Pray for the women who are thrown out of their Muslim families because of their stand for Jesus Christ. Pray that they will be able to find work to support themselves. Pray for the churches as they struggle to find ways to help and encourage these women.

- Pray that God in his mercy will bring peace and religious freedom to Sudan.

- Ask God for wisdom, strength and renewed hope for Sudan's pastors, who have to deal with overwhelming grief, trauma, horror, persecution, distress and despair. Pray for their ability to lead and nurture the church in the midst of this persecution.

- Pray for strength, grace and renewed hope for the Christians of Sudan, who are suffering profoundly.

- North African Christians and their families face continual harassment from the authorities. Pray for their protection.

- Pray for a hedge of protection from fundamentalist Muslims who see both Christians and Jews as infidels who have no right to exist. Pray for wisdom for Christian women in these hardest places as they search for the right ground between keeping their faith completely silent and being so vocal that they stir up the anger of those who would wipe out the church.

- Remember also the churches of the prosperous West. Pray that we will stand firm in our own faith and not be weakened and splintered by arguments and divisions. Ask God to allow us to grow into a mighty force with a voice that will resonate throughout the world on behalf of our suffering sisters and brothers.

North Africa
ACTION POINTS

- Learn about the individual countries of North Africa. Familiarize yourself with the people and the particular challenges they face, both culturally and politically. As you do, keep these words of Mehdi, from Morocco, in mind: "Our culture is different from yours. Americans have to learn to help without imposing their politics on our church. It's our work and our vision. If you want to help us, help us our way."

- Garner prayer and financial support from your friends to empower a health outreach for women in Senegal.

- Join a Sisters In Service trip to visit women's outreach ministries in West Africa. Short-term medical workers are especially needed. But even if you do not have medical training, you can document the work and report back to your women's group. Contact SIS for more information.

- With very few exceptions, missionaries are not allowed into North African countries. But Westerners with certain skills to offer (English teachers, computer technicians and programmers, medical personnel) can often get permits to go in and work . If they know how to be sensitive to the people and their needs, these workers can be a great help to local churches. Preparation and orientation with agencies that specialize in sending "tentmakers" is essential.

- Contribute to relief efforts that are keeping Sudanese Christians in refugee camps alive. One pastor said, "My people will not starve to death. We have brothers and sisters in the West; we are part of a family."

- Invest in literacy and microbusinesses for women in the displaced persons camps through the Sisters In Service network.

- For Mother's Day, in the name of a woman or girl you know, help at least one woman or girl in the Sudan camps by providing seed money for job training.

- Legislation that would target oil revenues Khartoum is using to fuel its war effort and to place sanctions on the government of Sudan has been endlessly stalled in both the Senate and House of the U.S. government. Let your congressional representatives know it must be passed.

- Make others aware of the suffering and oppression of believers in North Africa. It was largely because of the widespread publicity concerning the plight of the Soviet Jews, and the subsequent public outrage, that they were finally released from Soviet prisons. Make sure no one in your area can say, "But I didn't know."

- Work for the unity of the saints. We cannot think of ourselves as ministering in a particular country apart from the local Christians there. Serve their leaders in love.

PART 4

The Middle East

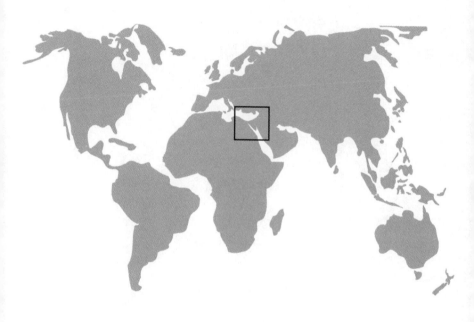

EGYPT

Population: 70,712,345

Religion: 94% Muslim (mostly Sunni), 6% Christian and other

Literacy Rate: Male 63.6%, Female 38.8%

Government: Republic

*O*ur country should be a Christian country!" Mena, an Egyptian woman, told us emphatically.

Up until the seventh century, Egypt *was* predominantly Christian—until the militant onslaught of Islam changed everything. Still, today Egypt is home to the Middle East's largest Christian community, somewhere between five and ten million people. And after the repression we had witnessed in North Africa, we were surprised at what seemed to be the country's relative religious openness.

"We are free to evangelize as much as we want, as long as we only talk to Christians," Mena reported.

What? Evangelize Christians? We were confused for days before we grasped a very important fact of religious life in Egypt: there is a big difference between *Christian* and *believer*. A believer is a person who knows and worships Jesus Christ, the Son of the holy and eternal God. The term *Christian*, on the other hand, has little to do with actual faith commitment. It is more a legal term for a community membership into which a person is born. People born into a Christian family are given a Christian name and legally marked as members of the

Christian community. They may have no interest in Jesus Christ—
they may not even *know* anything about Jesus—but it is safe to bring
up the subject with them because they are legally Christians.

Since Christians are considered second-class citizens, there are
many compelling social reasons to convert to Islam—a quick, easy process that is very much encouraged in Egypt. People born Muslim, on
the other hand, are strictly off-limits to Christians. The legal penalty for
proselytizing among the Muslim community is death. Even Muslims
who manage to convince authorities that they want to convert to Christianity of their own free will encounter all kinds of barriers and obsta-

cles. If they do convert,
they are greatly perse-
cuted; they may suffer
police torture and possi-
bly death at the hands of
militants—or even their
own families.

"I don't know what
percent Christian our
population is," one per-
son said in response to
our question. "All I
know is it is getting
smaller and smaller."

Kay Strom interviews an Egyptian Christian in Cairo.
[Photo - Lisa Ringnalda]

She is right. Until re-
cently, with the excep-
tion of Muslim converts, Christians were left in peace. Now that Islam
has been declared the state religion of Egypt, Islamic radicals are suc-
cessfully forcing a greater Islamization of society. Militant Islamic
groups are targeting Christians for assault, theft, extortion, even murder.
Because of this, emigration is high among Egyptian Christians. Also,
many who are born into Christian families but have no religious con-

victions convert to Islam because they want to marry Muslims or because it enables them to get job promotions and advancements that are not available to Christians.

Yet however quickly the Christian population is decreasing, it is not fast enough to suit the extreme militants. They are convinced that the problems in their society have been caused by the country's departure from the strict tenets of Islam. It is a dangerous trend, they insist, and can be reversed only by a return to a purer form of their religion.

Their cry, just the opposite of Mena's statement, is filled with rancor: "Our country will be a Muslim country!"

By Their Fruit
You Will Know Them

HABIBA'S STORY

*H*abiba sat straight in her chair and looked at us with gentle brown eyes. She was telling us about her friend Farza. "We met in the hospital when our sons were born. It's been awhile now—our boys are seventeen years old. Shortly after we met, I moved into a house owned by her father-in-law, so every month Farza came by to collect the rent, and she always stayed for a cup of tea and to talk. That's how it's been ever since."

Over the past seventeen years, Habiba and Farza have become very close. "She has seen me when I am sick, when I am happy, when things are going well and when they are not," Habiba said. "She has been here when my home is a mess and I would not let anyone else inside. Farza has seen everything as it really is. She is more like a sister than a friend because she knows so many of my secrets and I know so many of hers."

One of the secrets Habiba has shared with Farza is that she is more than just a Christian in name. She is a true believer, a follower of Jesus Christ. And although Farza is a Muslim, and although both women well know that by speaking together of such things they are committing the crime of "despising Islam," which is punishable by imprisonment, they talk.

Eleven years ago when Farza's husband left her with five young children and no money, she went to Habiba. They prayed together, and then Habiba helped her friend work out a plan whereby she could support her children. Habiba always stood ready to lend a helping hand with the little ones. It was not easy, but Farza made it. When she had trouble with her oldest son, she immediately headed to Habiba's house. Again they prayed. Her son's problem was settled, and he has never gotten into trouble again.

Just recently Habiba was awakened in the middle of the night by a frantic knocking on her door. It was Farza. Her youngest child was terribly sick and had been taken to the hospital.

"I just wanted you to be praying to your God," Farza said, "because your God is able to answer prayer. Whenever we tell him one of my problems in the name of Jesus, he makes things happen. Your God cares about me. Please, please pray for my little girl!"

Habiba did, and the next day Farza came to tell her the child was much better and would come home from the hospital the next day. When Habiba opened the door to her friend, Farza was standing with her shoes in her hand. In a quiet voice she said, "I cannot come into your home in my shoes, Habiba, because your home is a holy place."

Each time Farza came to Habiba with a new problem, Habiba would try to answer in light of what the Bible says. As time went on and Farza's trust in her friend grew, she began to ask extremely personal questions about her friend's religious life. Habiba always answered as honestly as she could.

"It is so hard here to talk to a Muslim," Habiba told us. "We cannot just tell our Muslim friends about Jesus Christ and see them become Christian believers. This is not the way it can be in Egypt. We must be willing to make ourselves vulnerable, to be sincere and open. We have to let people see that we have something they don't have. We need to let them know we can show them where to go for answers. It is not easy, and it is not something that happens quickly. In Egypt it is very, very dangerous to go to a Muslim and tell her about Jesus Christ. It is against the law, and the penalties for breaking that law are very severe."

"But you did talk to Farza about your faith," Michele said.

"Only because she asked me," Habiba answered. "If we are approached by a person and asked about the secret of our hope and why we are different, then we are told we are allowed to share. That's why it is so important that the people around us be able to see the difference in our lives."

Imagine having such pressure to live a life that is different. What a challenge! What, we asked, would be the marks of a life so quantitatively different that others would ask about it?

"Here in Egypt, a big one is in the family," Habiba explained. "There is unity in the family of the believer. There is faithfulness between husband, wife and children. There is love. Everyone really cares for the others. And for the woman there is stability and security. Christian men have only one wife, and they are faithful to her. How different from always worrying if you are going to be a second, third or fourth wife someday! This is one of the main things that brings Muslim women to us Christian women who are believers."

Although in many ways Christians are considered second-class citizens, they are also the ones who have earned trust. "Many, many times when a job requires someone who is trustworthy, a believer is chosen for the job," Habiba told us. "People really do recognize the difference in honesty and dependability."

Habiba, a proper middle-aged woman in a stylish suit and high-heeled shoes, sat before us with her hands folded in her lap. Could that be a tattoo on her wrist?

"Yes," she said. She showed us the Coptic cross tattooed on her right wrist. "Many of us Christians have these."

"Why?" Kay asked.

"Because we feel so certain that very severe persecution is right around the corner for us here in Egypt. And to be honest, if we are faced with the unthinkable, we do not know whether we will be able to stand up to it. Even Simon Peter, the apostle of Jesus, could not. We cannot abide the thought of breaking down and in a moment of weakness denying our Lord Jesus Christ. So we choose to have ourselves indelibly marked as his followers so there will never be any question."

We later learned that in angry frustration, militants have kidnapped some young believers and poured sulfuric acid on their wrists to remove their tattoos. The response? The determined believers simply had another tattoo applied on their arms above the acid scar.

Some wear the mark of their Lord on their wrists. But Habiba told us of their real desire: "We want everyone who sees us to see Christ in our eyes, in our humility, in our service, in our faithfulness and in our love. Then they will ask about the One to whom we belong, and we will tell them."

PRAYER POINT

Pray that Egyptian Christians will live in such a way that those around them will ask what it is that makes them different. Ask God to grant them courage and wisdom as they answer that question. (You may want to pray this prayer for yourself as well!)

16

Choosing the Hard Road

ADEL'S STORY

*W*e had learned the difference between *Christian* and *believer* in the Egyptian vernacular, but we still found ourselves confused. We had just finished talking to several women whom we knew to be active among the community of believers, and they insisted, "Persecution in Egypt? Oh, no! It is not at all difficult for us to live for the Lord in this country!" Yet when others spoke, they glanced carefully around to be certain no one was listening and then in hushed voices spoke of imprisonment, kidnappings, extortion, murder.

So as we sat with Adel in her home next door to the church her husband pastors in Alexandria, we asked, "What is the truth? How are believers treated in this country?"

Adel took a deep breath. Then, choosing her words carefully, she answered, "It is not difficult to live for the Lord in Egypt—if you minister to Christians. Our sisters and brothers in the early church were the ones who paid the price. It is not so bad now. Today we are free to worship. Bibles and Christian books are sold in Christian bookstores and churches and even on public bookstands. It is true that there are some restrictions on building churches and getting some of the higher positions. And some jobs are saved for Muslims. But we are good citizens and we pray for an atmosphere of peace, because we know we have to live and work together with all faiths. Some of the terrorists have aroused the anger of the people, and that ends up hurting all Egyptians, whatever their beliefs."

"So you are saying that Christian believers really do not suffer much persecution," we pressed.

"Not if they minister to Christians." Then she added, "Of course, over 90 percent of the population is not Christian, so that leaves them out."

"And what of them?" we asked. "What if you minister to them?"

For several moments Adel did not speak. When she did, it was in a heavy voice. "Conversion to Christianity from Islam is considered apostasy in Egypt," she said, "and shari'a law calls for a death sentence for that crime. For trying to convince someone to convert from Islam, the penalty is also death."

Twenty-two years ago, when Adel's husband started pastoring the church in Alexandria, he had no intention of doing anything other than working with the flock of Christian believers and reaching out to the surrounding Christian community just as his predecessors had done. And for five years that was what he did. But then a woman came into his office with three young children in tow, asking for help. She was Muslim and had left her abusive husband. "He will never look for me in a Christian church," she pleaded. "Will you hide us? Please?"

"My husband brought that lady and her children to our house," Adel said. "He talked to her about Jesus Christ and taught her from the Bible. She was our first Muslim convert. I was scared to death!"

Through the leading of the Holy Spirit and the loving guidance of Adel's husband, the woman converted to Christianity, and she insisted that she wanted to do it legally. When her Muslim name and her new Christian name were published in the newspaper, she began to receive death threats. She left the church with her children and went into hiding.

"What happened to her?" Michele asked.

All Adel would say was, "In all ways Egyptian law and the authorities favor Islam. Anyone who changes to Christianity here goes through a lot of suffering."

"You said this woman was the first Muslim to come to the Lord in your church," Kay said. "Does that mean there have been others?"

"Oh yes!" Adel said. "So many! Today much of our congregation is made up of Muslim converts." She told how her husband took immediately to reaching that part of the population few others were willing to touch. As for Adel herself, she was not nearly so willing.

"I was afraid for him," she said. "In fact I was fearful for all of us—we had two little boys. I would tell my husband, 'How do you know you can even trust this person?' I was so afraid someone would turn us in. Then one day a frightened young woman came to our door begging to see my husband, and he wasn't home. So she poured her heart out to me."

The woman was a new convert, and her angry Muslim parents were hunting for her. "Come and stay with us," Adel said. "We have a guest room. This house belongs to the church. You'll be Jesus' guest. Stay as long as you want. We can pray together, you and I or my husband, until we can find some way to solve your problem."

The young woman stayed for six weeks. After she left, Adel prayed, "Lord, make me available to others who are in need." In the years to come he made her available to many.

"When I myself experienced the joy of helping those people and seeing them come to a saving knowledge of Jesus Christ, I said, 'This is the way Jesus wants us to go, and he will be with us.' And that is true. He has been with us and he is still."

"So you're saying the authorities have left your husband alone?"

"Oh, no!" Adel said. "He has been threatened for the entire seventeen years he has been ministering. The authorities know him well. What's worse, the Islamic militants, who are quite active in our area of Egypt, also know him, and they would like nothing better than to have him disappear. But God gave my husband this ministry and no man can take it away from him. The ministry is growing and Muslims are coming to Christ. God *will* have his way."

It must have been difficult to raise children in an atmosphere of constant death threats, we noted.

"We could have stopped those threats, but the terms were not acceptable to us," Adel told us. "The fields were white unto harvest, and we were the workers chosen to do the reaping." Then she added with a smile, "Besides, this ministry was the means of our growing in our relationship with Jesus. Because, you know, it is through the tough times that we grow—as individuals, as a family and as a church. For it's when you can no longer depend on yourself or on each other that you are forced to finally depend entirely on God."

PRAYER POINT

Praise God for the joy he gives Adel and many others as they help others to meet Jesus Christ. Pray that we in the West may understand that our Lord will be with us whatever the persecution or hardships we may be called to endure for his name's sake.

17

Though It Cost Me My Life
ZORA'S STORY

*Z*ora's is the story of a woman who came out of Islam. Her new life started when she was twenty years old and met a Christian believer at work. She could immediately see by his manner and behavior that there was something different about him. When she inquired as to what it might be, he responded by slipping her a copy of the New Testament. That very night she started to read it. So moved and inspired was she that before she finished the four Gospels she herself became a believer in Jesus Christ.

Not one to be dishonest with her family, she approached them and said, "Please listen to what I have to tell you. I do not wish to disrespect you, dear family, but something very important has happened to me. I have been studying the Christian Bible, and I have found what it says to be true. Father and Mother, I am now a believer in the Christian religion."

"What!" her father roared. "You cannot be! I forbid it!"

"I mean you no disrespect, Father," she said, "but my conversion has already taken place. It is done."

As her mother wept and wrung her hands and her brothers called her terrible names and yelled out angry threats, Zora's father looked at her with a cold hatred that almost stopped her heart. "No daughter of mine would renounce Islam," he said in a stony voice she didn't recognize.

"Father, I . . ."

"Don't you ever use that term in my presence again! You are no longer my daughter!"

"The police will blame us for this!" one of her brothers insisted. "You will bring trouble on all of us!"

Again her father spoke: "If you want to leave Islam, then my sons and I will kill you."

For a minute Zora stood paralyzed, unable to comprehend the words that had just come from her own father's mouth. She couldn't have heard him correctly! But then her mother fell to the floor and lay in a heap, wailing in agony. She too had heard the pronouncement. As for her brothers, they were already preparing to jump on her.

There was no time to think, no way to reason with them. With one leap, Zora was out the door and running for her life.

In some countries Zora could have gone to the authorities, but not in Egypt. In many cases Egyptian authorities encourage families of converts to take care of "religious problems" like this one—and families often impose a more severe punishment than the police would.

Zora ran into a busy store, figuring the crowds of people around her would afford her some degree of safety. But once she caught her breath and her initial panic eased, she began to realize the extent of her predicament: she had no money, no identification, nothing but the clothes she was wearing. Where could she go? Certainly not to any of her relatives. If they had not already all been warned to be on the lookout for her, they soon would be.

She decided to telephone her best friend. So she borrowed money and dialed the number. To her relief, it was her friend herself who answered.

"Hello, this is Zora . . ."

"Oh, Zora, where are you?" her friend exclaimed. "Your brothers called and they are all so worried about you! Everything will be just fine. I'll come and get you. Tell me where you are and . . ."

Zora hung up the phone. She sank to the floor and held her head in her hands. They really were hunting her down! Her own family was going to kill her! And there was no one she could trust. Not a single person.

Well, maybe there was one person . . .

Zora borrowed more money and called the Christian believer from work.

"I told my family about my conversion," she told him. "Now they want to kill me."

"I'll be right there," he said.

When he came, he had a woman with him. "This is Josie," he told Zora. "She is a believer too, and she is visiting from Upper Egypt."

"I'm going home tomorrow," Josie said. "Why don't you come along? You can stay with me until you decide what you want to do."

With Josie's help, Zora was drawn into the fellowship of a church made up of people like her, converts to Christ from Muslim backgrounds. They encouraged her, discipled her and helped her find a job. Zora stayed with Josie for two months. Then she told her friend, "I will miss you, Josie, but it is time for me to be independent. I need to find a room to rent." And that was what she did. For the first time in her life, Zora was completely on her own.

It was six months before Zora dared contact her mother. Although they had a wonderful talk, her mother warned, "Your father and your brothers' anger is still hot. They vow that you will not be a Christian and live. Please, Zora, will you come home and be a Muslim again?"

Zora said, "I cannot do that, Mother. Not even for you. Jesus Christ is my Savior, and I must be faithful to him."

The next time Zora talked to her mother, her mother said, "I am very sick, my daughter. I may not live very long. Your father and brothers will be gone from home all next week. Will you come and visit me for just a few days? It would help me so much to see your face again."

Zora's new friends warned her not to go. "It could be a trap," they said.

"But it might not be," she replied. "I don't think my mother would lie to me. I can trust her."

They all gathered to fast and pray; then they sent Zora on her way. "I will be back in two days," she promised.

As soon as Zora stepped into her parents' house, her brothers sprang out of a back room and bolted the doors behind her. Then her father entered and ordered her to kneel before him.

"I will be merciful," her father said. "You may repent and once again become the Muslim you truly are."

"No, Father," Zora said. "Do whatever you have to do. But what I am is a Christian, and that is what I will stay."

For several minutes Zora's father stared at her in silence. Finally he said, "We will say no more tonight. Tomorrow we will settle this disgrace to our family once and for all." Then he turned and left the room.

In the middle of the night, while the family slept, Zora managed to squeeze through a tiny window and make her escape. Then she found her way back to Upper Egypt where her friends lived.

Zora never saw her family again. Twice she called her mother, but both times her mother's tone was accusing and threatening. The last time she told her daughter, "Don't call me again. You no longer have a family."

"My mother is wrong," Zora says. "I have a wonderful family. I have sisters and brothers all over the world. And I have a Father in heaven who is worthy to receive power and riches and wisdom and strength and honor and glory and blessing forever and ever. What more could I ask?"

PRAYER POINT

Pray for those whose families turn against them because of their faith in Jesus Christ. Ask God to draw them especially close and to let them know they have a worldwide family.

PALESTINE

Population: 4,355,725 (combined in Israel, the West Bank and the Gaza Strip)

Religion: 97% Muslim, 3% Christian

Literacy Rate: Male 91.5%, Female 77%

Government: Because Palestine is not a country, there is no official government. There is an uneasy dual government by Israel and the Palestinian Authority.

*P*alestine—Arab or Jewish?

Or Christian?

What? What does "Christian" have to do with Palestine?

Actually Christianity has a long history in the land, and it is not restricted to the time of Jesus and the days of the early church. Once a Roman province, Palestine under Byzantine rule was transformed into a Christian country, with Jerusalem as its glittering metropolis. This lasted from the middle of the fourth century to the middle of the seventh century, when the Arabs conquered the area. Palestine attained spiritual prominence in the Christian world during those three centuries, and materially it was a prosperous time for the province.

Today, in the ongoing and increasingly heated controversy over who has a right to the land, the "time immemorial" argument is used frequently. Many Arabs contend that since Palestine has been occupied continuously by Arabs, it belongs to them by right. Certainly there is a great deal of room to argue this basis of ownership. The Jews have an entirely different line of reasoning: the land was a gift bestowed by God on Abraham's descendants, and it had to be won by conquest from the Canaanites. Yet since the "time immemorial" argument continues to be brought up, it is good to remember that Christians too have been a constant presence in the land.

Many Westerners will be amazed to know there is a good-sized community of Palestinian Christians whose presence is a living link between us and the earliest Christians, and their line has continued to live in the land for over fifteen hundred years.

18

The Baker's Daughter
RANDA ALEA'S STORY

Randa Alea, the baker's daughter, was born in the Old City of Jerusalem—the very same place, she loves to say, where Jesus ministered and died. There were five children in her family, and Randa was the one right in the middle.

The Alea home was Eastern Orthodox. They all did their best to be as good as they could be—"good" being defined by their home and school. "It was never clear to me from what I was taught that I could have a relationship with God through Christ," Randa said. "As a girl, I knew God was big and loving, but I was afraid of him. We were taught that if you do good you will go to heaven."

Randa's teen years were exciting. She belonged to the Orthodox youth club and attended its activities—something like Girl and Boy Scouts in the United States. "You might wonder how children and teens can manage to have fun when they live in a constant atmosphere of civil unrest," she said, "but they do."

Although turbulence and upheaval were always present, the intensity went in cycles. "Our lives were interrupted many times," Randa said. "Stores and shops would close down, and life would come to a standstill. We were taught that we were to be people of peace, even though we ourselves were often under attack. So my friends and family, and the other people at church, refused to join the demonstrations. However, many of the public school kids didn't hesitate to show how they felt. For instance, on the way to school we would see a pile of tires burning in an intersection. That was a way for Palestinians to show their frustration at constantly living under siege."

Randa's family's home was located in a dangerous area between Jerusalem and the West Bank. "But in God's kindness, in 1967 we moved to the suburbs where it was safer, just fifteen minutes from the Old City," she said. Having outgrown their house, they had been able to move to Biet. "Although we were in a better place, our schools were still located right in the middle of the problem area."

When an attack came, Randa ran with others from her house to the safety of a shelter. "Though we had stores of food at home, there was no time to collect any of it," she said. "We went for five days with next to nothing to eat. When things settled down and we felt brave enough, we finally risked making our way back to our home. Imagine how we felt to see shattered glass everywhere, and bomb fragments on our beds."

Although she was just a child, the trauma of returning to her shattered home after the bombings is indelibly seared into Randa's memory. "Our mother tried to feed us, but no one wanted to eat," she said. "She finally gave up and went to work cleaning up the glass. What else could she do? Life goes on." It took about a month to move beyond the trauma and get back into the pace of daily life.

When Randa's baby brother was only six months old, there was another attack and the family had to run to a shelter once again. One man had been wise enough to build an underground basement for his family, and everyone in Randa's neighborhood, as well as the neighborhood adjoining it, ran and took refuge there. There were around forty people crammed into that shelter. Everyone was safe, but there was no food and no place to sleep.

"If you were fortunate, your mother would have a small blanket for you," Randa said. "But my mother's concern was for my baby brother. She sent my father back to our house two treacherous blocks away to get the baby's crib."

A mother in this war-torn region would constantly be on the watch.

144 DAUGHTERS OF HOPE

Would her children make it home from school? Was it worth risking one parent's life for a child's well-being? Was it possible to keep the home normal when the world had gone crazy?

"Whenever there was a major upheaval, there would be no way for the children to get home," Randa recalled. "Even on normal school-days, the buses had to go through Israeli checkpoints to be checked for terrorists. We never knew what to expect."

The day finally came when Randa's parents had had enough. Randa remembers it well: "My father was upset when he came into the house. Something had happened, but he wouldn't tell us what. 'Why should we always live under worry?' he thundered. 'Why should we suffer the indignity of always having our privacy invaded? Why should we put up with people forever telling us what to say and do?'

"We did not care about the fight for land. We were not interested in material things. The family, the children — that's what was important to my parents."

Randa's father's frustration coalesced into a plan. The family could move out of Palestine but keep the house. That way, one day when things settled down they could return. The parents began to talk with excitement to their five children about the great opportunity they could have for an education in America.

In the end, everyone moved to the United States except the oldest child, who was not allowed to leave the country with the rest. "My mother could barely stand it," Randa said. "Imagine how she felt, leaving her twenty-one-year-old daughter behind with all those dangers. My sister stayed alone in our home. We had an uncle and cousins living next door, but it was horrible to leave her." One year later, however, she was able to join the rest of the family in the United States.

Randa's life changed dramatically when the family immigrated. Because she was the most fluent in English, she assumed the role of head of the household. She found the family a house, selected schools for her siblings and enrolled them, then learned to drive. "I didn't have time to be upset about our situation," she said. "I had too much responsibility."

The move was extremely difficult for Randa's parents. Her father had been a respected caterer, a chef for the royal family. But in America he couldn't even get a small bakery going.

And yet the move was to change their family for all eternity. In 1983 Randa's sister was invited by her manager at work to attend a Bible study. At first she refused, convinced that it would not be in line with her religious upbringing. But her manager was persistent. Eventually she attended and enjoyed it very much, even though some things she learned were different from what she had been taught. At home she spent hours searching the Scriptures, determined to discover if it was true that a person could have a personal relationship with Jesus Christ.

"I remember hearing my sister crying and praying in her room at night," Randa said. "It confused me. I would ask her, 'Why does this new religion make you so sad?' But my sister explained that she had an indescribable joy and an assurance of heaven. She cried and prayed, she said, because she could not bear to think that her family wouldn't be with her forever."

Randa and her family could not help but notice that the sister's entire life had changed. And because of what they saw, one by one she and her parents and siblings all came to know the Lord. "When my parents decided to be baptized, it caused a kind of warfare in the extended family," Randa said. "For a time everyone disowned us. Eventually, though, the family opened up to us, and now we all get together. We're just longing for the day when they too will come to Christ."

Randa is dismayed at how many Christians in the United States have no idea that there are Christians in the Arab world. Certainly there are Arab Christians, just as there are Jewish people who have come to Christ. These Christians are living and dying for their faith. They make up a tiny minority right now—only 3 to 5 percent of the Arab Palestinian population is Christian. That is because so many have left the region to find safety, jobs and a simple, peaceful life for their children.

"Most churches in the United States teach such a strong pro-Jewish point of view that they forget there are Arab Christian brothers and sisters who also need their help and prayers," Randa said. "Please remember that of course there are Palestinian Christians. Palestine was where Jesus grew up, and many people followed him there. Why would there not be Palestinian Christians?"

And she has one more thing to say: "God has brought healing on the inside to our family and to me personally. My hope is not in Palestine. I live wherever God chooses for me to live on earth, because my true home is heaven."

PRAYER POINT

Thank God for the remnant of Christians in Palestine. Ask him to allow them to be a unique redemptive force in their region.

The Middle East
PRAYER POINTS

- Pray for the young believers of Egypt, that they will develop a deep relationship with the Lord that will withstand the wiles of the evil one. As one Egyptian woman said, "Satan is at work in the world and in this country. What hope do our children have without prayer?"

- There are willing and gifted women leaders within the Egyptian community of believers, but they face resistance in some of the traditional churches. Pray that God will allow the entire body of Christ to work together so that many souls may be drawn into the kingdom of God.

- Pray for the believers of Egypt who must consistently live lives that are wordless testimonies to those around them. Pray that the fruits of the Spirit will show forth in such a way that those with whom they come in contact will be compelled to ask what it is about them that is so different.

- There is great poverty in Egypt, and many Christians struggle simply to find enough to eat. New converts from the Muslim faith suffer the most. Remember to uphold them in prayer for their physical needs.

- Pray that Egyptian believers will see the importance of marrying within their faith.

- Once a Christian becomes a Muslim, it is very difficult to move back again. Pray that Christians will be able to resist the many enticements the government dangles before them to convert them to Islam.

- Pray that God would reveal to the church in the United States the truth about their Arab sisters and brothers in Christ.

- Pray for the peace and safety of Jerusalem and the troubled regions surrounding it.

The Middle East

ACTION POINTS

- "Egypt, the leader of the Arab world, looks up to America," one woman told us. "We need you to keep the faith in your country. Do you in America understand the responsibility you have?" That point was stressed to us over and over, in country after country. We Western Christians must keep our faith strong and maintain our ability to speak for our Christian sisters and brothers around the world. Besides speaking up for religious freedom and praying about it, we must consider it when Election Day comes and it is time to cast our votes.

- Many Arab Christian women reinforced the link between their witness and the behavior of Christians in the West. "It does terrible damage to Christians who are risking their lives when nonbelievers can point to the decadence of American Christians. Please remind the women and girls to dress modestly, to be kind to others and to show generosity."

- Training programs for Arab Christian women to serve as directors of women's ministries in seventeen nations are under way. Approach the director of women's ministries at your church to see if your women would like to sponsor the training of Arab sisters. Contact Sisters In Service for details on how to do that.

- Strengthen the outreach of Egyptian Christian women by praying for and helping to fund portions of their programs.

- Talk to children (yours or others') about Jerusalem and Palestine in Jesus' day and now. Lead them in identifying the area on a map. Help them to understand that they have Christian brothers and sisters in nearly every country of the world. Talk to them about our responsibility to the suffering members of the body of Christ.

PART 5

The Most Dangerous Places on Earth

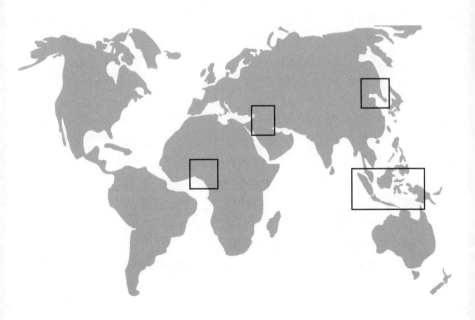

INDONESIA

Population: 231,328,092

Religion: 88% Muslim (mostly Sunni),
8% Christian, 2% Hindu,
2% Buddhist and other

Literacy Rate: Male 89.6%, Female 78%

Government: Republic

We're going to be in India and China," I told my dinner guests, one of whom, Silvani, was a young woman I had just met. She had recently arrived in this country from Indonesia. "And we are planning to go to Indonesia too. I'm looking forward to your telling me about it."

"Oh," she said, "where are you going? To Java, where I'm from?"

"No, to North Sumatra." I told her the name of the city.

Silvani's hands flew to her face, and she let out a terrified cry. "Don't go!" she cried. "Oh please, don't go! You don't know what it's like! You could be killed there!"

The rest of us stared at her in shock. "But Silvani," I said, "it couldn't be that dangerous. Half the population there is Christian."

"That's exactly what makes it so dangerous!" she exclaimed. "In the areas where the Muslims feel the most threatened, that's where they are the most aggressive and militant."

We didn't go. And Silvani was right. As it turned out, shortly afterward that particular area exploded into deadly violence.

By law, the Indonesian government allows its citizens to follow whatever religion they choose. But in reality Muslims get preferential treatment and protection. As in many other Muslim-influenced countries, the Islamists' stated goal is to eliminate Christianity from the nation. To that end, Indonesian churches are being destroyed and believers persecuted and tortured in terrible ways. Christians are being kidnapped and forcibly converted to Islam. In some areas military forces have been involved in the attacks and killings.

Yet despite tremendous persecution, the church in Indonesia continues to grow. In the past forty years the number of evangelical Christians has increased from 1 million to 11.5 million.

19

To Live Is Christ, to Die Is Gain
MIRAH'S STORY

*T*he ranting village shaman was running right at Mirah. In a second his machete would fall on her neck. Mirah raised her small hand in front of the shaman's face and commanded, "In the name of Jesus, stop!" The man stopped in his tracks, his arm went limp, and his weapon dropped to the ground.

Mirah was in yet another unknown village, and once again she was confronting the dark forces that hold many people captive in ignorance and fear. This small, middle-aged Indonesian woman's ministry is filled with miraculous interventions such as this. How did she become so bold? How is it that God reveals himself in such powerful ways to support her work? The answer is in her simple journey of faith and faithful determination.

Empty-nest syndrome affects many women of Mirah's age. She had already raised her children to adulthood while faithfully supporting her husband's ministry. With that behind her, she needed to step back and consider how best to invest her time and energies. An important part of her exploration, Mirah decided, would be to attend the Evangelical Theological Seminary of Indonesia. Perhaps there God would speak to her heart and let her know what he wanted her to do.

She excelled in her classes and became more and more certain that God was using her studies to prepare and lead her into a new phase of ministry. As she neared her final semester, she began to contemplate what would be her biggest assignment of all. To graduate from ETSI, students must plant a viable church, fully functioning and with elders in place. Mirah's concerns over this challenge sent her to her knees in prayer. "I prayed that God would lead me to just the right place and help me to plant the right church."

As she prayed, Mirah felt compelled to ask her professor to assign her to the most difficult place in which to plant a church. She wanted to go to a location where no one else was willing to go.

At first her professor dismissed the request. "I know of such a place," he told her, "and it is not too far from here. But no one can plant a church there. Not only are the village leaders hostile to any outside influence, but the entire region is far too dangerous. And you—well, you are a woman. It would not be safe." He went on to describe the area in order to prove just how inappropriate it would be.

From his description, Mirah knew exactly the place her professor was talking about, and she was more certain than ever of what God was asking of her. He wanted her to extend the love of Jesus to the "impossible" people of northern Sumatra.

Mirah began making short trips to one village at a time in an area that had never before heard of Jesus Christ. Her strategy was simple: she would visit a home and ask if the people inside would like to have God bless their home. The response was always the same; she was immediately, though cautiously, brought inside. Everyone was nervous. They motioned for Mirah to be quiet while they closed the windows and drew the curtains. Once everyone was seated, Mirah would explain that God loved them and wanted to bless them and that he had made a way for their sins to be dealt with and forgiven through the blood of his own Son, Jesus. What a blessed relief this good news offered from the fear and spiritual oppression in which they lived! Nearly everyone with whom she spoke prayed to receive Jesus.

On her next trip to each village, Mirah would visit the same homes in order to instruct and encourage the new believers. To her amazement, she would find those houses filled with extended family members. The believers would beg her, "Please tell my father and mother. Please tell my sister-in-law. Tell my family what you told us the last time you were here."

In that most impossible of places, where no one could plant a church, where the village leaders were too hostile—and even though Mirah was "just a woman"—a church grew.

Mirah graduated in more ways than one.

"From the day I began going to these people I felt a deep burden for them," Mirah said. "They were captive to oppressive, superstitious leaders. Many of the people were in bondage to spirits. They wore charms around their necks for protection from harm. It was a miserable way to live. I knew that Jesus came to set the captives free, but first they needed to be told about him. When I was not doing this work, I was weeping for the people. So it was better for me to go, even though I knew danger waited for me every day."

Indonesia is an archipelago of over thirty thousand islands. Much of Mirah's work involved sloshing through mucky areas or paddling a small boat to get from one island to another. "My heart was always broken when I would see the people," she recalled. "No clean water, no electricity, no schools—only poverty and fear."

Wherever she went, Mirah always took supplies: oil and lamps, paper and pencils, cassette players, tapes and batteries. But she soon outpaced her ability to supply what was needed for each village. "I began to train others, starting with young Indonesians who were willing to teach on a remote island," Mirah said. It was a lonely and hard life for her coworkers. Mirah realized that she would have to support the workers financially, emotionally and spiritually. So once a month she started to hold retreats for all the workers in her ministry. It was a time to get away from the pressures of the ministry in an area of Sumatra where Christians could sing out loud in safety and be encouraged by the Word of God. For all of them, it was a time of spiritual refreshment.

"Many of them cried when it was time for the retreat to end," Mirah said. "The pressures in that area are so very great. But I tell them that they have to leave, and I have to leave too."

When small churches began to grow, community leaders aggressively pressured the believers to renounce their faith or get out of the area. Not long after Mirah's work began, leaders of the entire region became determined to expel all Christians. Each village leader went house to house demanding that families either renounce their faith or leave their homes and villages. Imagine Mirah's dismay when five thousand refugees appeared outside her home.

Immediately Mirah went to work to rent houses for the people. "We had five or six families in one small house," she said. "Each family got one room. If it was only a couple, they lived in a closet." She also rented land. "The people needed to work, so I bought farm tools and seeds for them to plant."

Eventually many of the refugees went back to their homes. And when they did, they went back stronger than ever, equipped to work together to shine the light of God's love on those who had persecuted them.

Mirah's ministry and vision continues to be innovative. She has now established a seminary on the border of the difficult area in which she ministers, and it is regularly turning out Indonesians who take up the calling to plant churches in unreached villages. She also has a thriving radio program that broadcasts in the tribal language of the people. And ignoring warnings and threats against her life, she continues to lead evangelistic events.

One time when Mirah and a small team made a return visit to a remote village, they were immediately surrounded by a crowd of angry people, some carrying machetes. "We knew we were in serious trouble," Mirah said. "They started accusing us of contaminating their people. We tried to explain that we did not come to cause trouble, but that just made them angrier and more hostile."

Someone yelled out that Mirah and her group should be killed to keep them from coming back. Just then the town's jailer heard the commotion and came to see what the problem was. He immediately took them into protective custody. Then he turned to Mirah and told her in no uncertain terms that she had better give him some assurances that would calm the crowd outside the jail.

"God sent us to tell the people about his love," Mirah said. "We must obey God and keep coming, even if it means we might die." Then, looking straight at the jailer, she said, "We are not afraid to die today, but we are very worried about you, sir. If you are killed along with us, what will happen when you stand before God?"

The jailer hesitated. "But we still have these angry people outside," he said.

"If God wants to save us, he will," Mirah told him. "We know that people are praying for us. We have Christians praying for our safety, Christians in Jakarta, even Christians in the United States."

This news delighted the jailer. He promptly went out to the crowd and began negotiating for the release of the prisoners. After three full hours of negotiations, the crowd dispersed. They were afraid of sparking an international incident.

A small, very ordinary and seemingly powerless group of women in the United States had "adopted" Mirah and her ministry. They supported her financially, emotionally and spiritually, and most of all, they were earnestly committed to prayer. They were the American Christians who were praying for her safety. God used them that day to save the lives of Mirah and her team on the other side of the world.

Mirah is under no illusions about the danger of her calling. She says: "I know I might die here one day. I have already come close many times. I have been stoned, hunted, threatened and arrested. But I am not afraid. If I die today, it will be my day of blessing to see Jesus. If I don't die, it is only because Jesus has more for me to do here. Either way, I am fine."

PRAYER POINT

Thank God for choosing to use the small, ordinary and seemingly powerless to accomplish his work. Pray that God will use us to enable our sisters in the difficult places to serve him more fully.

IRAQ

Population: 24,001,816

Religion: 97% Muslim (60% Shi'a, 37%
                     Sunni), 3% Christian and other

Literacy Rate: Male 70.7%, Female 45%

Government: According to its constitution, a
                     democratic republic with a 250-
                     member parliament. But as of this
                     writing, a repressive dictatorship
                     has been removed. The country is
                     in transition.

*I*raq is a land steeped in biblical history. Abraham was born here. It was to this country that the Jews were taken as captives, and the prophet Daniel served the kings of Babylon here. And it was through this land that apostles traveled on their journeys between Jerusalem and India.

Today there are few Iraqi Christians, most of them in the Chaldean Christian community. They have been afforded a place in this overwhelmingly Muslim society—so long as they remember that the power of God must never attempt to rival that of the president. After Saddam Hussein came to power in 1979, Christians experienced increasing trouble. For example, it became illegal and extremely dangerous for them to have Bible studies or prayer meetings in their homes.

Outside of Iraq, the largest Chaldean community is in Detroit, Michigan. As this book was being written, the ongoing international sanctions against Iraq and the unsettling threats of war were driving increasing numbers of Christians to use their family connections to immigrate to the United States in search of a brighter, more secure future. The conversions within the country cannot keep up with the number of people who leave. This trend only increases the Islamization of what was once a relatively secular society. More and more women in Baghdad do not go out without fully covering themselves with chadors. And in many neighborhoods the streets are empty of women after dark.

It is not an easy time to be a Christian in Iraq.

And yet . . . a Christian Iraqi sent word of Amira, a Christian Kurdish woman who had recently lost her three daughters in a car accident. Amira's husband blamed his distraught wife for the accident, insisting it had happened because she converted to Christianity. He took her to court to make her pay for her crime of conversion.

In front of everyone, the Muslim judge asked her, "Do you believe in Jesus Christ?"

If Amira had been from the Christian community, answering the question would not have been particularly dangerous. But she was known to have been a Muslim. She well knew that a Muslim who had turned her back on her faith would be shown no mercy. She would be in great trouble if she answered yes to the judge's question. At the very least her baby son, her only surviving child, would be taken from her and given to her husband to be raised as a Muslim.

Still, Amira stood up and bravely proclaimed, "Yes, I am a Christian. And I have a right to choose the faith I believe in."

To everyone's amazement, the judge replied, "Yes, you do have that right. Keep your son until he is sixteen years old. Then he will decide for himself which religion he will follow."

"What, then, shall we say in response to this? If God is for us, who can be against us?" (Romans 8:31).

20

With Love to Iraq

ZADAH'S STORY

During the Gulf War in 1991, Zadah's husband had the least enviable job a conscript could hold in the Iraqi army. He was a radio tower operator. "Imagine my husband praying to God to save his life as the American pilots targeted his tower!" she said. God did spare Natan's life, again and again.

"One of my most vivid memories of those awful days was of taking my children grocery shopping. I remember holding their little hands and zigzagging in between heavy artillery and massive tanks—just to buy milk."

The ending of the Gulf War only stirred Saddam's hatred to a higher pitch. The world watched in shocked horror as the regime rained oppression and killing down on the Kurdish population in major Iraqi cities. He was determined to rid Iraq of their presence.

Throughout the world there are thirty million Kurdish people, and they are mistreated and despised wherever they go. In fact they are the largest people group without a nation of their own.

One night as Zadah and Natan were sitting down to dinner with their family, they heard the thundering of helicopters. They hurried outside to see what the commotion was all about. To their horror, they saw that the poverty-stricken Kurdish neighborhoods were being bombed. Rivers of people were pouring out, running toward their more exclusive Iraqi neighborhood. Men and women ran with children in their arms. Young men carried their grandmothers on their backs.

"We could not understand why these people were so hated," Zadah said, "but we knew right then we had to do something to help them." Zadah and her family started secretly helping the Kurds to survive, ministering to them with food, blankets and love.

"Watch out," their friends warned them. "If you aren't careful, Saddam will turn his wrath on you."

Under the unrelenting pressure, the Kurds began an exodus to the no-fly zone, which offered them an umbrella of safety. There are now four million Kurds in the provisional territory known as Kurdistan. They struggle to survive in that rugged area where everything is in disrepair—roads, water systems, electricity, schools for their children.

"More and more, we were becoming convinced that God wanted us to help the Kurds in a more substantial way," Zadah said. "But we couldn't do it from where we were. It would mean leaving our home and extended family." That would be a huge sacrifice. As educated people, Zadah and Natan enjoyed a very high standard of living. Their children had known nothing but a privileged life. How could they pick up and move their family to live in the no-fly zone?

Twice the Lord impressed on Zadah's heart that she had to make a decision. That moment of decision finally came on an ordinary day as she was walking down a busy street. Zadah recalled, "I heard someone ask, 'Zadah, what are you going to do?' I looked around, but there was no one talking to me. I knew it was the Lord. In that moment all my possessions passed before my eyes: my beautiful home, the furnishings I so treasured, my clothes and jewelry, our cars—so many nice things that we owned. I humbly answered, 'I will leave everything to follow you, Lord.'"

That was Zadah's moment of freedom. There on that busy street, a torrent of joy poured down from heaven and flooded over her. As she went home and began packing a small bag for each member of her family, her joy only grew. "We gladly handed over the keys to our house and our cars to our neighbors," she said. "We knew we would probably never return."

The family left at night and made their way through numerous checkpoints before finally arriving in Kurdistan. "We had just enough money for a few months of survival," Zadah said, "but we were so happy to begin our ministry." They started their outreach with those who had been most hurt by war, the thousands of people who were left handicapped and impoverished. Zadah worked with the handicapped women, many of them widows, teaching them simple handicraft skills. But Zadah's and Natan's burden for the people increased, and soon their ministry extended to show God's love in other ways.

Zadah tells how "angels" from the United States began to help by supplying them with ministry equipment and medicines. "We saw that if we would boldly step out to minister, God would supply what we needed."

There are now well over five hundred Christians in five major cities of Kurdistan. Many are working together to extend God's love.

The vision to bring the transforming power of God's love grew to include schools. "This was a risky proposition," Zadah says. "We needed a permit to build a school, but the governor of Kurdistan is a teacher of the Qur'an. We didn't know how he would respond to our proposal."

After much prayer the couple approached the governor. They respectfully explained that they were able to teach and were willing to set up a school for children but that they were Christians. Their plan was to offer an alternative school with an English certificate from the United States. They would teach Kurdish children their heritage and that they are loved children whom God created.

"I will permit this, but only if you will allow my children to attend your school," the governor told them.

They were overwhelmed. The need for schools is so great that they were granted not only one permit but four.

The first school began functioning in February 2001 and would serve as a model for the next three. The families involved have been delighted with the changes they are seeing in their children. In fact several of the fathers asked whether there might be something for their wives as well.

In Iraq a man may legally have four wives. This is a painful reality for Iraqi women. "Women are unhappy and afraid to complain about this situation. Although many women are abused, some men truly love their wives and want the best for them," Zadah said.

"God gave me a vision for a center for women," she said. "Purity and family honor are very important issues in this culture, and women are extremely limited as to where they can go and what they can do. They need a place of their own." The Ruth Centers for Women will offer women a place where they can come together and bring their preschool children. "The women can sit in the bookstore/coffee shop and talk to each other," Zadah said. "They so need a loving place to unburden their hearts and ask questions. We will also offer them other opportunities— to learn to use a computer, for instance, or to exercise. Right now this is just a vision, but we're trusting God for what we need to bring these centers to life."

To talk to Zadah is to see and hear her passion for the Kurdish people. "Women are dying every day without knowing that God loves them," she says.

One new Christian told Zadah about the loss of his Muslim wife. "My wife was a good woman," he told her. "She was a faithful wife and the mother of my children. Because of her, I never wanted more than this one wife." One day his wife was in their house. She had just washed her hair, which was very thick and beautiful. So she opened a window to allow the warm air to blow through her hair as she combed it. She did not realize that her husband's father was walking in the courtyard nearby the open window.

"When my father saw my wife's beautiful hair, it inflamed a murderous anger in his heart against her," the man said. "He came to me and told me I must kill my wife for causing unclean thoughts in him."

The man refused, even though his father demanded he kill his wife to save his honor.

One day while the man was at work, his father and brothers came into their home, took his wife by force into the mountains and killed her. There was no recourse. She was only a woman.

With tears running down her face, Zadah said, "That man's wife was murdered for brushing her hair in her own home! If something isn't done, there won't be any women left up here!"

Women suffer so much. Must they suffer without knowing there is a God who loves and treasures them?

PRAYER POINT

Pray for women whose culture and religion allow them no rights or value. Pray that the Ruth Centers will become a reality for the Kurdish women of Iraq.

AFGHANISTAN

Population: 27,755,775

Religion: 99% Muslim (84% Sunni, 15% Shi'a), 1% other

Literacy Rate: Male 51%, Female 21%

Government: Transitional

*J*he way of the *Pashtun*," it is called. The strict unwritten code requires vengeance for insult and values honor above life itself. It also requires its women to stay shrouded and secluded from public life. We in the West caught a glimpse of how harsh and uncompromising that way can be in the aftermath of the attack of the hijacked planes on the Twin Towers of the World Trade Center and the Pentagon on September 11, 2001. Before that most of us could not even have located Afghanistan on a map. Now it is seared forever into our hearts and minds.

Since that notorious morning we have learned many things about this desolate, mountainous country in central Asia. But few of us know that there is not only a growing church in its capital, Kabul, but also small clandestine Christian congregations slowly spreading in the country's isolated villages. There is even word of Christian groups that are quietly worshiping Jesus Christ in mosques in some of the remote areas—although they must be extremely circumspect in doing so.

And the ranks of believers are swelling. Christians who had fled to refugee camps in Pakistan during the horror days of the Taliban are coming back across the border. People inside the country are hearing the gospel via Christian shortwave radio stations broadcasting in the principal Afghan languages, Pashtu, Dari and Farsi. It's impossible to know how many are tuning in.

For generations the way of the Pashtun has been a part of the patchwork that makes up Afghanistan. But it may not be long before we are hearing mention of "the way of the Christian."

21

Tell Me the Stories of Jesus
BAHIRAH'S STORY

*I*t is the holy month of Ramadan, and Bahirah has her house decorated and has finished preparing the special holiday foods just as her neighbors have. Even though she and her family are Christians, it is too dangerous not to do such things.

"Of necessity, we largely remain out of sight," she says. "We do what we can to blend in. It is just one of the difficult compromises we must make in order to survive here."

Bahirah sits on the *dari,* the mat covering the floor in the women's part of the house. Men do not enter here, just as women do not enter the men's area. Her husband is not at home, however. He has left for a Bible study class in Peshawar, a five-day walk one way. He has heard about a correspondence school for Muslims who want to know more about Christianity, and he hopes to find out more about it.

"I do not feel at ease when he is away," Bahirah says simply. She need not say more.

The number of Christians in Afghanistan is very small. Christians who allow their faith to be known face extreme persecution. Employers will not abide Christian employees. Authorities levy heavy fines on Christians. Christians constantly face imprisonment, and their families are threatened. The only schools are Muslim schools, so Christian parents must either send their children there, knowing they are receiving Muslim instruction, or teach them at home.

Muslims who dare to convert to Christianity are subject to unspeakable persecution. "The official punishment for converting is what we call *sangar*," Bahirah said. "That is death by stoning."

Both Bahirah and her husband are converts from Islam. She first heard about the Christian God over a shortwave radio. When her husband found her listening to it, she was terrified of what he might do. But to her amazement, he sat down and listened alongside her, and he too was drawn to the message he heard. Later an American soldier gave them a Bible in their language, smuggled in from Pakistan. Today a house church meets in their home.

"There are four of us who come together to worship Jesus Christ," Bahirah says. "The others are married to Muslims who do not know they are Christians."

What is it about Christianity that would cause an Afghan woman to convert and risk execution?

"Oh, the stories of Jesus!" Bahirah says. "His miracles! He made blind people see and lame people walk again. He even raised the dead to live again! The first time I heard about a religion that heals, I could not stop listening. The Christian God is a God who cares. That's what makes the difference."

PRAYER POINT

Pray that the women of Afghanistan will be able to hear the stories of Jesus and know the Christian God who truly cares about them.

NIGERIA

Population: 129,934,911

Religion: 50% Muslim, 40% Christian, 10% traditional ethnic religions

Literacy Rate: Male 67.3%, Female 47.3%

Government: At this writing, Nigeria is transitioning from military to civilian rule. There are wide differences between the cultures of the more feudal, predominantly Muslim north and the largely Christian south.

*A*s the millennium changed, international eyes were on the country of Nigeria. It was just beginning a full year of democratic government following a long military rule. That was good news, since it had known only one decade of an elected government since leaving the British empire in 1960. There was also bad news, though. The year 2000 also saw the rise of Islamic fundamentalism as several of the states in the north moved to implement Islamic shari'a law. The result has been terrible and deadly conflicts between Muslims and Christians that have threatened to permanently divide Africa's most populous nation.

"Our constitution guarantees to every citizen freedom of conscience and religion, recognizing that we are not only citizens of one country but also children of one God," said President Olusegun Obasanjo, himself a committed Christian. Yet he has been sorely criticized by some of his fellow Christians for not being harder on the militants who were intent on imposing shari'a law.

Archbishop Olubunmi Okogie spoke for many Christians when he insisted that a dual system of government would not work and went ahead to say, "Nigeria is not an Islamic country."

The killing goes on, especially the killing of Christians.

There are bitter stories of persecution coming out of Nigeria. In fifteen recent years over thirty major religious conflicts were recorded in the northern part of the country. In these conflicts thousands of people were killed and hundreds of churches were destroyed.

Most analysts believe life is going to get increasingly hard for Christians under shari'a law. Yet many believers are certain that President Obasanjo has been placed in his position for such a time as this.

22

Under Grace, Not Under Law

AMAKA'S STORY

$\mathcal{L}$ife is about to get tougher for non-Muslims, especially Christians, in the northwestern Nigerian state of Zamfara, as new measures are rolled out to enforce Islamic (shari'a) law, first adopted two years ago.

The wearing of turbans and veils by male and female students in post-primary institutions will now be compulsory, the state's education commissioner, Umar Ango Bakura, told reporters in the state capital, Gusau.

He stressed that there would be no exceptions.[1]

Turbans and veils? No exceptions? It was hard to picture that.

Only months before, we had met three wonderful women from Nigeria at an international Christian women's conference. They were from three different Nigerian states: Zamfara, Kaduna and Kebbi. All three states are now under shari'a law. The three women were dressed in brightly colored outfits and wearing lipstick and rouge. Amaka had said, "Just look at us! Can you imagine us living under shari'a law?"

We laughed and talked and took each other's pictures. They asked us to pray for the political future of their country. But they also expressed great hope and their belief that a committed Christian could be in the presidency

---

[1] Emman Usman Shehu, "Nigerian State Gov't Implements New Anti-Christian Measures" (January 29, 2002) <www.CNSNews.com>.

Nigerian Christians at the women's conference. [Photo - Kay Strom]

only because God had placed him there. "There is no other explanation," Folami said. "There are more Muslims than Christians in Nigeria, and the Muslims would have done anything to stop it if they could have."

"He's going to bring change to our country," Jummai agreed. "But he is a wise man. He is not going to move too quickly. He is not going to tear the country apart."

"Perhaps a nation like ours is hard for you to understand," Amaka told us. "We are many different people, and we all have our own ways. It is not easy to make many ancient nations into one modern one."

Amaka, Folami and Jummai told about the work they did in Nigeria. In two of their states, house fellowships had been banned and many church buildings had been destroyed. So the women went from house to house, encouraging other Christian women, holding prayer meetings and organizing Bible studies. They also held regular Sunday school for the children. When we asked about their husbands, however, our friends fell silent.

The next afternoon I (Kay) wandered early into the near-empty auditorium and saw Amaka sitting alone, so I went over and sat beside her. We exchanged pleasantries, then commented on how nice it felt to just sit and relax. We were silent for several moments. Then Amaka said, "Shall I tell you my story?"

"Yes. I would like to hear it."

"I am from the state of Kaduna, right in the middle of the Islamic militants' stronghold. They fight hard to control our state, even though 70 percent of Kaduna is Christian. Christians have been terribly persecuted where I live. Girls have been kidnapped and forced to marry Muslim men, which makes them legally Muslim. If they try to become Christian again, they are killed, because that is the penalty for a Muslim who converts to Christianity. Now Christian leaders are arrested and jailed, and all evangelism is strictly banned. In our state three hundred churches have been burned to the ground."

Amaka's eyes filled with tears and she paused, overwhelmed by her memories.

"You asked about our husbands," she said. "Let me tell you about that. Folami's husband disappeared the night his church was burned. She doesn't know if he was kidnapped or killed. Jummai's husband is in jail. My husband was murdered by a mob that came and pulled him out of our house and beat him to death."

She looked at me, tears streaming down her face, and said, "Please, do not think we hate living under shari'a law because we cannot dress the way we want or we cannot be like you Americans. No, we hate it because of what it does to our people. Do you know, there are thousands of homeless Christian widows and orphans who have no place to go. Their homes have been destroyed. Horrible things are being done. Tell me, what kind of law is that?"

Amaka told of one village where Christians were awakened early one morning by the ringing of church bells. They got up and made their way to the church, thinking it was time for prayer, only to be ambushed and shot by Islamic militants.

"They shoot us as we pray and burn our churches to try to keep us from worshiping," she wept. "That is not law!"

I reached over and took Amaka's hand, and we sat and wept together.

The singer for the evening was starting to rehearse on the stage below us.

Amazing grace! How sweet the sound
That saved a wretch like me!
I once was lost but now am found,
Was blind but now I see.

"We are Christians!" Amaka said. "We will stay Christians, and we will continue to work for our Lord. No one will force us to do anything else. No matter what they do to us, we will be Christians."

Through many dangers, toils and snares
I have already come;
'Tis grace hath brought me safe thus far
And grace will lead me home.

PRAYER POINT

Remember the compassion of your sisters in the difficult places of the world, who do not ache for the lack of material goods but for the suffering of their fellow believers. Pray for the homeless, suffering, persecuted Christians of Nigeria.

NORTH KOREA

Population: 22,224,195

Religion: Traditionally Buddhist and followers of Confucius; 1-2% Christian. Autonomous religious actions are almost nonexistent. The government does sponsor religious groups to give the illusion of religious freedom.

Adult Literacy: Male 99%, Female 99%

Government: Authoritarian socialist; one-man dictatorship.

*I*t is difficult to imagine a harsher, more repressive country than North Korea. It is difficult to name a place filled with more misery.

Famine has become a way of life in North Korea. United Nations officials estimate that between 1999 and 2000 more than a million people died of malnutrition-related diseases. So desperate are the people that many risk their lives in an attempt to sneak into China in search of relief. If they are caught, they are heavily fined and immediately sent back. Or their legs are broken and they are dragged back. Or wires are put through their wrists and they are hauled back. The message is clear: Let this be a lesson to anyone else who might be tempted to try to escape.

A returned person must endure intense interrogation to make certain he or she has not been contaminated by any bit of Christian influence. If so, that person is condemned to a labor camp or given a death sentence. Christianity will not be tolerated.

Before the end of World War II, when Korea was partitioned into two countries, there were an estimated three thousand churches. But the Communist government promptly closed most of them. Hundreds of thousands of Christians fled to the south before the border was sealed upon the outbreak of the Korean War. In the years that followed, under increasing persecution, most others are believed to have abandoned religion, although no one knows for sure. Estimates of how many Christians there are in the country vary from ten thousand all the way to three hundred thousand. There are even whispered reports of a large, silent underground network within North Korea, though many others doubt that. What everyone does agree on is that it is a colossal understatement to say, "It is not easy to be a Christian in North Korea."

23

How Can They Hear?

PARK CHOI'S STORY

$\mathcal{E}$arlier in the day I (Kay) had spoken to a large group at a church in downtown Seoul, South Korea, and now it was nice to be sitting comfortably on the floor around the table in a well-appointed apartment. Since we were on the thirty-fifth floor, we had a spectacular view of the university city where I was staying. I had been listening with interest to the conversation as best I could. I had been invited by a group of women committed to intercessory prayer. They were all wives of university professors, and their husbands had joined us around the table, along with their minister and his wife.

Someone mentioned North Korea and how committed South Koreans were to praying for the reunification of the country. "We don't care what it would mean for us economically," she said. "They are our brothers and sisters."

"Does anyone know anything about the Christians in North Korea?" I asked.

Everyone exchanged glances. No one said a word. I figured I must have said the wrong thing, so I busied myself with my chopsticks and bowl of rice.

Then Pastor Lee, who sat next to me at the head of the table, cleared his throat. Everyone's attention was immediately focused on him.

"We don't talk about Park Choi," he said to me, "but since you are going back to America, and since you are a writer, maybe it is good for you to know."

Park Choi was born in North Korea in 1955. Her family were Christians. They never had the luxury of attending a church. Instead, at night the family would all lie down on their sleeping mats and, huddling under the blankets, whisper the Christian hymns her parents and grandparents taught them. Then they would recite Scripture together and pray. Over and over, Park Choi's father reminded the children to whisper in the softest of voices. If any prayer or words of Scripture were overheard, they could all be killed.

Park Choi's grandfather, though, could not contain himself. One time he actually sang out loud. Park Choi's mother was so upset she couldn't stop shaking. She said, "If we're caught, we will just disappear. Who knows where we will go? It could be to prison or it could be to be shot or hanged." They told the grandfather he could not even whisper the hymns anymore. From then on he was only allowed to move his lips.

As Park Choi grew up, she understood that her mother had good reason to be afraid. Since the year she was born, approximately three hundred thousand Christians have disappeared. And she could see why they spent so much time memorizing Scripture. Anyone found with a Bible could be shot on the spot.

Park Choi did not know of any other Christians. That did not mean she did not *know* any; she just didn't know *of* any. Many years later she discovered that a friend she had known her entire life was a believer, but it was kept so quiet that they never knew about each other's faith. The way Park Choi discovered it was that her friend was arrested one day and shot the next.

Pastor Lee stopped talking, so I asked, "How did you find out all this about Park Choi?"

"She told us," Pastor Lee said.

In the terrible famine that has gripped North Korea, Park Choi watched first her parents and then her two young children starve to death. In desperation, she and her husband managed the dangerous escape to China, and from China they made their way to South Korea.

"It was an amazing feat!" Pastor Lee said. "It was as if she escaped prison and found herself in paradise!"

That was how they knew her. She and her husband had come to their church. The stories the two of them had to tell horrified the listeners: the terror, the torture, the suffering. This woman and her husband had never before worshiped with any Christian believers other than their own family—not ever! There was wonder on their faces when the congregation stood and sang hymns out loud. Tears fell when they heard God's Word read right out of the Bible. It was almost too much for them to bear. They sobbed uncontrollably throughout the service.

"You in South Korea are so missions minded," I said. "You go and live and preach among the people who have treated you the worst because you care so much about their souls. You even send missionaries to the United States. Aren't you able to do anything to help the Christians in North Korea?"

"We try," Pastor Lee said. "We are always ready to help any defectors who make it to the South. We maintain a secret way station in China to help people like Park Choi make it here. And we smuggle in Bibles so tiny they are not likely to be seen. We also send tons of food and supplies to help keep people from starving. Oh, and we broadcast a radio program into the North. We have had some very good reports from that."

North Korea has built a couple of churches and erected a seminary building, but it is commonly agreed both are done merely with an eye to appeasing the West and securing financial assistance. There is little if any religious substance to either of these projects.

"Other countries criticize South Korea and say that North Korea is fooling us and just doing this to extract money from us," Pastor Lee said. "But we are not the fools others take us to be. We know this is Kim Jong's game. But we have to do what we can. God just asks us to be faithful. He will take care of the results."

"I would love to have the chance to meet Park Choi," I said hopefully.

"That is not possible," Pastor Lee answered. "She is no longer here."

"No?" I asked. "Where did she go?"

Park Choi's husband got a job at the church, and they had a nice apartment close by. They had so much food to eat they had stomachaches every day. Never before in their lives had they had the luxury of deciding when to stop eating. Everything seemed to be perfect for them. Except Park Choi knew something wasn't right.

She began to wonder: How could they continue living in such comfort and ease when the people they had known and cared about all their lives were dying without ever having so much as heard the name of Jesus? It was nothing short of a miracle that they had both made it out of North Korea and into China, then that they had made it out of China and into South Korea. Could it be that God only intended this to be a training ground for them? That he never really meant for them to live here?

She turned to the Bible for guidance. There she read: "How, then, can they call on the one they have not believed in? And how can they believe in the one of whom they have not heard? And how can they hear without someone preaching to them? And how can they preach unless they are sent?" (Romans 10:14-15).

Park Choi took the verses to her husband and told him what was on her mind. To her amazement, he said he had been thinking the same thing. So now what they had to do was even more impossible than sneaking out of North Korea—they had to sneak back *into* North Korea.

"Every year for a few days the road is opened from the South to the North so that people can take food to their relatives," Pastor Lee said. "The last time the road was open, one of our relief workers saw Park Choi. So that she would know we haven't forgotten our part, he said to her, 'Remember, you are sent.' We are still praying for her and her husband every single day."

PRAYER POINT

Pray for the believers in North Korea. Pray that the ongoing famine and terrible hardships will give Christians an opening to offer eternal hope to the people of that desolate country.

The Most Dangerous Places
PRAYER POINTS

- Pray for the Christian community in Indonesia, that they might have strength and increased faith and grace in these difficult times. Ask God for wisdom for their leaders. Pray that the witness of the church will lead many more to Christ.

- Remember in prayer the Christians in Iraq who have suffered greatly and are continuing to suffer. Pray for their efforts to extend God's love.

- Pray that God will use this critical time in Afghanistan, when new laws are being considered and a new constitution formulated, to bring religious freedom. Pray that the church may be able to witness and grow and bring hope and healing to Afghanistan, and that this country might become a force for reform and moderation in central Asia.

- Pray for Nigeria's Christian president, Olusegun Obasanjo, as he strives for peace and order in a nation divided by religion. Ask God to raise this country up to be a force for stability in Africa.

- Pray for the estimated one hundred thousand Christians who are being held in North Korean labor camps, where they face starvation, torture and death.

- Christians of North Korea are in a perilous situation. Pray for their protection as they go about the Lord's work. Also pray that the gospel of Christ can be heard in that country and that it will be received.

The Most Dangerous Places
ACTION POINTS

- Find northern Sumatra on a map of Indonesia. Touch it with your finger. Tell two people this week that you touched the place where a courageous Indonesian empty-nester woman works.

- Commit yourself to helping one outreach in northern Sumatra this year. Support a student, pay for radio airtime for Mirah's ministry, provide ministry travel money.

- Create an advocacy group for Mirah. We can put you in touch with her for regular updates. Use that information to inform others and to garner prayer and support for this growing work.

- Five women are needed to come and teach English to the teachers in the new schools in northern Iraq. Perhaps you or someone you know is interested. If so, contact us.

- The Ruth Centers for reaching Kurdish women with God's love will remain a vision until the resources are provided to build and equip them. Might you trust God to help supply these resources through a network you have?

- The recent war has fragmented the infrastructure of Iraq. Now is the time to pour love onto those who fear that Christians in the West are their enemies.

- Put into practice Christ's commandment to love your enemies, both personal and international.

How Shall We Then Live?

I (Kay) belong to the Good Stewards Investment Club, ten Christian women who get together the first Tuesday of each month and make modest joint investments in the stock market. This is never going to fund our retirement, but we are learning about the world of finance and we have a good time together.

Last month we were lamenting the continuing sag of the stock market. Usually when it comes to complaining about a bear market, I'm right there with everyone else. But this time I was deep into the stories for this book, and as the women around me talked investments, all I could see were the faces of my serving, suffering sisters.

When there was a lull in the conversation, I commented, "All this talk about women in business and making investments makes me think about Mehdi, a woman I met in Morocco . . ."

"Really?" the president of the club asked. "Tell us about her."

So I did. I began by telling how women who come out of Islam are literally thrown out of the house by their husband, then disowned by their family. I told about the tiny church that tried so hard to support the new Christian women who had come, but everyone was so poor they just could not do it. I told about the Sunday morning when they came together to worship the Lord and found their sister in Christ lying on the path. She had starved to death. I told them how Mehdi had sobbed out the church's horrifying decision to look the other way as the women did the only thing they could to earn enough to keep them alive—work as prostitutes. Then I told them Mehdi's question that had haunted me since that day: "What can we do? Tell me, what can we do?" I had no answer for her.

The club members stared at me in silence. No one moved.

"But they did find another way," I said. Then I explained the church's plan of setting the women up in business.

When I paused for breath, the woman next to me said, "I move we take the eight hundred dollars we have accumulated in our treasury and invest it in setting all the women converts in the Moroccan church up in business."

"No!" I said. "I can't take all that money and just send a check over there to Morocco!"

"I second the motion," another woman said.

"Wait a minute!" I said. "I wouldn't even know where to send it! We can't do it like this!"

"Why not?" the president chimed in. "What could be a better investment for our money than putting it into the lives of Christian women? Now that we know about their plight, we want to help."

We finally settled on a decision to tithe our investment money for the women, and I was to find out where to send it by the next meeting.

Now that we know, we want to help. That is the response we have heard from women and men again and again, all across the country.

We have now heard stories of women from the Near East to the Middle East to the Far East to Africa and Indonesia. We have met the women. And so the question is: How will we live from here on out?

Let us suggest four ways to live: as people of knowledge, as people of the gospel, as people of prayer and as people of action.

PEOPLE OF KNOWLEDGE

When Najma told about her daughter dying in the fire, I thought I would never get that horrifying picture out of my mind. And I never believed I would be able to recall Zhang Yuan's crushed feet without tears flowing from my eyes. My mind, I was certain, would forever reel at Mehdi's story, and the picture of Songa forced to leave her babies in order to follow her Lord would be with me forever.

When I got home from my trips, I could think of nothing but the sto-

Part of our group sits in a Beijing hotel listening as Chinese women tell us their stories. Michele Rickett is third from the left; Kay Strom is fourth from the left. [Photo - Rachel Johnston]

ries I had heard. The faces of those women were constantly before me. When I prepared meals, I weighed in my mind every spoonful of food against the meager fare of my sisters. I could not abide the waste that is common in our society—and I probably said that a few times too often to too many people. And in those first days and weeks back home I was amazed—and even a bit hurt—by friends who seemed to have no interest in trying to understand what I had experienced.

"We all suffer for Christ," one woman said. "Just today someone at work shot me a rude glare because I wouldn't listen to her offensive jokes."

Even at church, the response was often, "But on the whole, was it a fun trip?" As if I had been on a cruise.

But time passed. The piles of work waiting at home distracted me from my thoughts about the women. There were appointments to keep and people to meet. Very soon there was another book to start. Before long, several days could go by without my shedding a tear or even uttering a prayer for those sisters who had moved me so profoundly. What was wrong with me? How could I forget so quickly?

We cannot—and should not—remain totally buried in someone else's suffering. But we also must not allow our everyday world to crowd out what we have seen and shared in these pages. Knowledge brings responsibility. Perhaps that's why it makes us so uncomfortable. Once we know the weight of our sisters' burdens, we must shoulder them and carry them as our own (Galatians 6:2).

But the fact is, those burdens are quite unfamiliar and they lie quite uneasily on our backs.

When we were in Beijing, a woman challenged us: "You Americans think life is supposed to be pleasant. When it's not, you think something is wrong. You have to fix it so you can be happy and comfortable again. You have not learned to trust God when life is hard. You have not learned the lesson of finding his purposes for you when you are uncomfortable. You have not yet learned to find joy in suffering."

I can't say we appreciated hearing that, but she was right. If we are honest, we have to admit that few of us like moving outside our comfort zones. We are not used to living where things are unsafe and where there is no security. We can hardly abide ridicule; it is almost impossible to even conceive of risking torture or death for the sake of the gospel.

You may find that your new knowledge will make you uncomfortable with "business as usual" in your home church. That is because in many American churches the emphasis has turned inward to a quest for personal satisfaction and happiness. Many churches have become places where people come first of all to be healed, to rid themselves of guilt and stress and anxiety—a place to mend their relationships with others and to work on their self-esteem.

Funny thing, though. In all his ministry, none of that is what Jesus stressed. He put his emphasis on the physical needs of others and, more important, their spiritual needs. Since he came to fulfill the law and the prophets (Luke 24:44), consider what the prophet Micah wrote about the desire of God's heart:

> He has showed you, O man, what is good.
>> And what does the LORD require of you?
> To act justly and to love mercy
>> and to walk humbly with your God. (Micah 6:8)

We have a responsibility to move out of our comfort zones, however uncomfortable that may make us, and become women and men of knowledge. Do not let your quest for information end with what you have read here. Continue to learn more about your sisters (see <www.SistersInService.org>). Many women find it especially encouraging to get together regularly to share information and pray with others who have a heart for women serving in the hard places. An advocacy group may be just the thing for you. There are guidelines on the Sisters In Service website for starting such a group.

PEOPLE OF THE GOSPEL

"To live as true Christians," Wu Chein had told us, "to be like the Master, is not easy anywhere."

That's just what Jesus said to his disciples: "Remember the words I spoke to you: 'No servant is greater than his master.' If they persecuted me, they will persecute you also" (John 15:20).

"Our eternal life caused Jesus to come down from heaven and suffer on the cross and give his life," Adel, the woman from Egypt, said. "So why should anyone think the Christian life will be easy? Believers who truly follow Jesus Christ will be persecuted because Satan is always against Christ, and he will be until the Day of Judgment. Christians anywhere in the world are going to be persecuted some way if they walk right and refuse to compromise. That's what Jesus said."

People of the gospel are people who are willing to share in Christ's suffering. But what of us who worship in comfort and freedom? It would be foolish indeed for us to take what we have for granted and to ignore what our sisters are experiencing. Or, for that matter, for us to forget those who went before us and suffered sorely so that we can enjoy our comforts and freedoms. We know from history something of the horrors they suffered. Hebrews 11:36-38 tells us:

> Some faced jeers and flogging, while still others were chained and put in prison. They were stoned; they were sawed in two; they were put to death by the sword. They went about in sheepskins and goatskins, destitute, persecuted and mistreated. . . . They wandered in deserts and mountains, and in caves and holes in the ground.

And here is what the passage says about such people: "The world was not worthy of them" (verse 38).

Adel told us that at times she would begin praying for a person to come to the Lord and, worried about the person's ability to endure, would pray that the person not be beset by the horrors that can confront Egyptian converts to Christianity. But things did not work out as she prayed. Certain that the Holy Spirit was leading her, she could not understand why there seemed to be so many problems bombarding the person. Then, she said, she would begin to realize that it was no favor to be allowed to come easily to the Lord.

"I need to talk to that person, to nurture and encourage her. And I have to keep praying for her," Adel said. "There is a price to be paid. Not the price for our salvation, of course. That's been paid. But the price of sharing in Jesus' suffering."

She is right. "Everyone who wants to live a godly life in Christ Jesus will be persecuted" (2 Timothy 3:12).

"Jesus also suffered outside the city gate to make the people holy through his own blood. Let us, then, go to him outside the camp, bearing the disgrace he bore. For here we do not have an enduring city, but we are looking for the city that is to come" (Hebrews 13:12-14).

We tend to skip over those words, because while we do want to live a godly life, we don't want to be persecuted. We do not like the idea of "going outside the camp" and bearing abuse. We like staying inside the camp where we are accepted and it is comfortable. We love the idea of the city to come, but we are also pretty fond of the city right here. We know what Jesus bore, and we don't want to go with him and bear it too.

In India we had just listened to a group of Dalit women tell of the harsh persecution they had endured because of their stand for Christ. Before we parted I (Kay) asked our usual question: "Is there anything you would like to ask us?"

They looked at me curiously, shyly. Before we came, none of them had ever seen a North American woman.

Finally, through the translator, one woman said, "Did you ever go hungry because you're a Christian?"

"No," I said. "I never did."

"Did you ever have your house taken away?" asked another.

"No," I said. "No, I didn't."

"Did you ever lose your job because you're a Christian?" inquired another.

I shifted uneasily in my seat. "No," I said.

"When people find out you are a Christian, do they throw rocks at you?"

"No. No one throws rocks."

"Has anyone ever thrown you in a fire because you are a Christian?" It was the first woman again, and she was leaning forward eagerly awaiting my answer. I did not have to ask the source of the scars on her own dark brown arms.

"No," I said. "You see, in America those things don't happen. In America it's against the law to throw people out of their houses or take away their jobs or stone them or throw them in the fire because they are Christians."

The women stared at us uncomprehendingly. Then one said, "But if it doesn't cost you anything, how do you in America know what it means to be a Christian?"

As I was thinking about how to answer, the first woman asked, "If you in America did have to suffer, would you still be Christians?"

I took a deep breath and answered her honestly: "Some of us would and some of us wouldn't. We need you to pray for us that when we face persecution, we will have the strength to stand up under it as you do."

"We will pray," the women promised solemnly. "You tell people in America that we in India are praying for them."

People of the gospel know that living a godly life means sharing in the suffering of Christ. And they are willing, with God's help, to stand up and be counted among the saints throughout the centuries who have done so. We are in this world to be about the business of extending the good news of the Father's love where it has not gone—whatever the cost.

PEOPLE OF PRAYER

Every one of us is to be a person of prayer.

Here is a wonderful model for praying for our distant sisters and brothers. The apostle Paul writes this to the Christians in Rome, far away from Jerusalem:

> I thank my God through Jesus Christ for all of you, because your faith is being reported all over the world. God, whom I serve with my whole heart in preaching the gospel of his Son, is my witness how constantly I remember you in my prayers at all times; and I pray that now at last by God's will the way may be opened for me to come to you.
>
> I long to see you so that I may impart to you some spiritual gift to make you strong—that is, that you and I may be mutually encouraged by each other's faith. (Romans 1:8-12)

It is important that we be consistent in praying for those who live and labor faithfully for Christ in the hard places around the world. It does not matter whether or not we have met face to face. We do know *of* their faithfulness, because it has been reported to us. The more we know about them, the more we will be encouraged to pray regularly and specifically. And as we consistently lift our sisters up to God, our love for them will grow deeper. But the benefit does not end there; as we encourage our distant sisters through our prayers, we will in turn be encouraged by their faith.

If prayer were a mere practice in obedience, that would be sufficient reason to pray. But it is far more than that. We have a God who hears and answers prayer. Just look at some of the wonderful promises that are ours to claim:

> Before they call I will answer;
>> while they are still speaking I will hear. (Isaiah 65:24)

> Call to me and I will answer you and tell you great and unsearchable things you do not know. (Jeremiah 33:3)

> Again, I tell you that if two of you on earth agree about anything you ask for, it will be done for you by my Father in heaven. For where two or three come together in my name, there am I with them. (Matthew 18:19-20)

> Therefore I tell you, whatever you ask for in prayer, believe that you have received it, and it will be yours. (Mark 11:24)

With promises like these, how dare we *not* be people of prayer?

PEOPLE OF ACTION

In Luke 12:42-48 Jesus tells a parable about a great master who appoints a manager over his servants and entrusts him with their well-being until his return. If the master returns and finds the manager faithful, Jesus says, the master will reward him greatly. But what of the manager who abuses his responsibility? In the parable he is punished severely, beaten with many blows. Jesus explains the parable with these sobering words: "From everyone who has been given much, much will be demanded; and from the one who has been entrusted with much, much more will be asked" (verse 48).

We live in comfortable homes—houses or apartments, condos or mobile homes—with refrigerators and pantries stocked with food. Even the most needy among us is not without resources to meet daily needs. Our fight is not against malnutrition; it is against overindulgence.

No one beats us or stones us or throws us into a fire because we are followers of Christ. There is not one of us who cannot have a Bible if we want one—and in any language we feel comfortable reading. There are churches whose doors are open to us, and ministers are welcome to preach from the Bible. If we want further scriptural teaching, it is readily available to us in countless books that can be purchased in stores or online or through the mail or checked out of the public library or accessed on the Internet. There are correspondence courses, Bible schools, cassette tapes, radio preachers and teachers, and endless other resources.

We are blessed indeed. But, make no mistake, with such blessing comes great responsibility.

It is easy to get overwhelmed and cry out, "Wait! There is so much need! I cannot do everything!"

No, of course you can't. None of us can. We can't feed all who are hungry and bind up all who are broken and ease the suffering of all our sisters and encourage all the weary and fund all the worthy projects that need money. We cannot do it all.

But each one of us can do something.

"You don't know me!" you may be protesting. "I truly am not in a position to do much. I can pray, and maybe I can give a little money. But I'm really not a likely person . . ."

Wonderful! God delights in using the most unlikely among us to accomplish his work. In India we were asked to speak before a group of almost two hundred Dalit Christians. These were women who, after generations of being told they were the lowest of the low, were just beginning to grasp the idea that they actually have true value and purpose in God's eyes. We recounted the story of Esther, the lowly Jewish captive who was mightily used by God in the ancient land of Persia. Through the courage and faithfulness of that one young woman, he prevented the slaughter of the entire captive Jewish population.

If you had asked Esther if she was capable of such a job, she would surely have exclaimed, "No! Absolutely not!" And she would have been right. But consider her uncle Mordecai's words to her: "If you remain silent at this time, relief and deliverance for the Jews will arise from another place, but you and your father's family will perish. And who knows but that you have come to royal position for such a time as this?" (Esther 4:14).

Through God's empowering, Esther did the job. And that's how it is with us. God has put each one of us in the time and place we are, with the blessings and circumstances we have, for such a time as this. As with Esther, perhaps the most powerful thing you can do is to speak up about the sufferings of others and keep working on their behalf. Trust God to take the steps you can make and infuse them with light and life to make him known.

Prepare to be amazed at what God calls—and then equips—you to do! Why? So that everyone—including you!—will know it was God, and not you, who accomplished it (1 Corinthians 1:25-26).

So what can you do? Well, you can . . .

• *Organize Kingdom Prayer*
In Egypt and Morocco we were impressed with the coming together of believers in regular, concentrated sessions of kingdom prayer. In Morocco believers met once a month and prayed all night. This is a regular feature of the church in South Korea as well, a church that has experienced phenomenal growth and vitality. We are convinced that it is also

an important key to strength in the church of North America and in our ability to positively affect the world for Christ.

On arriving home, Kay and her husband, Dan, started a one-hour prayer time at their home one night a week, modeled after the prayer time in Egypt. During this time they asked people not to pray for friends and neighbors who were ill or for personal problems, but to limit the hour to prayers for the furthering of God's kingdom and the strengthening of the body and of Christ's church at home and around the world. They tried to be specific in guiding the prayer time, keeping in touch with ministries and leaders in other countries, praying for believers in areas of the world that are affected by world events, praying for Christians who live and minister in the hard places.

It is not as easy as it sounds. People are far more eager to pray for their own personal concerns than for unseen sisters and brothers around the world. They need someone who is informed and will persevere in leading and encouraging them and in giving them specifics for which to pray. They need someone like you.

• *Share the Stories*
Through the past years as the two of us spoke at conferences and retreats, telling stories of our sisters in the hard places, many people came up afterward and begged, "We need stories we can tell too! We haven't been to these places or met these people like you have, but we need the stories!"

Well, now you have them. You have stories of inspiration and courage and hope right at your fingertips. We want you to make them your own and share them. Use them to educate others in your church, your organizations and your community. Share them with your friends so that they too will become impassioned about our sisters around the world.

We invite you to make the women in this book your personal friends. Make their plights your cause, their needs your mission. Help us make

Western women aware of their sisters who live and serve God right where they are.

We remind you, of course, that the stories are under copyright, so you cannot just copy them and reprint them in your newsletters. But you can use the ideas and retell the stories in your own words, and we encourage you to do so.

• Make Your Sisters a Part of Your Church

In one good-sized church in a good-sized city in Michigan, everyone follows the news about the accelerating hostilities in Indonesia with one name foremost in their minds: Mirah. They all know her. They have read her letters, they have her picture hanging on their refrigerators, and when she came from Indonesia they piled into the church to hear her because they could not wait to meet her personally. Everyone there prays for Mirah, from the tiny children to the senior citizens. She is their sister and they care deeply about her. On the front of that church is a sign that reads: "PRAY FOR THE CHRISTIANS IN INDONESIA."

Are there sisters who are a part of your church—*really* a part, the way Mirah is a part of that church in Michigan? Is there a sign on your church to remind passersby of Christians who are laboring in the hard places?

How about your church newsletter? Is there a regular column dedicated to the believers who struggle and suffer persecution to make Christ known?

• Make Your Vote Count

Why would Chinese women ride three days in a cattle car from Mongolia to meet with women from America and ask them to pray?

Why would women in Egypt, Morocco and Tunisia appeal to us to pray first and foremost for the moral purity of our American churches?

Why would a woman in Indonesia credit having American friends with keeping a mob from harming her?

Why would Nigerian women risk flying to Houston to a conference just weeks after the attack on the World Trade Center towers?

Why would a pastor in South Korea tell the story of the escaped North Korean to an American writer?

Because America has great power and influence throughout the world. We saw that again and again, in country after country. "The fear of angering America is the only thing that keeps us from being wiped off the face of the earth." We were told this several times, in different words, across North Africa. And repeatedly women pleaded, "Please, please, don't forget us."

We can put pressure on our government to insist that nations that want to have a good relationship with us stop persecuting Christians. We must not sit in silence while our country turns a blind eye and pretends nothing is happening. We have access to our representatives in Congress, and we can make our concerns and opinions known. It is vital that we be aware of issues that arise and that we immediately respond by writing letters, e-mailing or placing telephone calls. When elections come around, know where the candidates stand on such issues, and vote accordingly.

• Stand in the Gap

When we were in India, a group of Dalit women were just beginning a course of training that would teach them to read and then instruct them in the Word of God so that they could serve as Bible study leaders in their villages. The woman in charge of the program confided, "I am concerned about these ladies. They just aren't as strong as other groups have been. I don't know if any of them can make it through the course. Will you pray for them?"

"Not only will I pray," I said, "but I'll ask my Bible study group to pray too."

My Bible study group of ten women considered it an honor to pray for the women, and they took the commitment seriously. After six weeks we got an e-mail from India telling us the news: every single woman completed the course! "What wonderful things can happen when you superior people pray for people like us," the leader wrote. We were shocked at those words but touched at the loving appreciation we received for the gift of six weeks of concentrated prayer.

These became our women. We bought materials for them, we followed their progress, we got pictures and short biographies of them, we sent them information about us. Most of all, we prayed earnestly for them. They had become a part of our group. "If they need anything, you let us know," we told our contact, and she did.

The Bible tells us that there are places and times when those in power act like lions tearing into their prey, devouring everything in sight. At such times, the Lord looks for someone to stand in the gap and intervene on the people's behalf (Ezekiel 22:25, 30). Who is better situated to do that than impassioned American Christians, informed and armed with prayer?

Imagine the day when we stand before God's throne and the Son of Man in all his majesty and glory announces: "I was hungry and you gave me something to eat, I was thirsty and you gave me something to drink, I was a stranger and you invited me in, I needed clothes and you clothed me, I was sick and you looked after me, I was in prison and you came to visit me."

You stare in confusion. The Almighty One is blindingly glorious. Unforgettable! Yet for the life of you, you cannot remember ever having met him before. There has to be some mistake.

You fall on your face and say, "Lord, when did I ever see you hungry or thirsty? When did I see you a stranger or needing clothes? When did I see you sick or in prison? When did I ever minister to you at all?"

Then the Most High leans forward and looks at you earnestly. In the most loving and tender of voices he says: "I tell you, my child, when you did any of these things for the least of these sisters of mine, you did it for me" (Matthew 25:35-40 paraphrased).

SISTERS IN SERVICE

Strengthen the weak
Satisfy the oppressed
Speak up for the voiceless

OUR MISSION

To inform, mobilize and equip advocates to extend God's love to the least reached, least valued: women and children.

WORKING IN THE HARDEST PLACES

Afghanistan	India	Mali
China	Indonesia	Senegal
Egypt	Iraq	Sudan

EQUIPPING THE LEAST VALUED

We work to empower women through practical grassroots projects, led by our courageous sisters. The lives of destitute women and children are transformed now and forever by initiatives of health, education, economic and spiritual life development.

Through our advocacy ministry, we share the harsh realities with people who have the resources and freedom to strengthen the weak against poverty, disease, exploitation and spiritual darkness. We invite ordinary people to serve as SIS advocates by becoming champions for one particular place or project.

In our troubled world women and children are least fed, least educated, abused, abandoned, abducted and enslaved. They comprise:

80% of refugees	80% of unreached
70% of the poor	4 million trafficked
2/3 of illiterates	2 million endure female mutilation, 500,000 die each year

Though they are the least valued, women hold the most powerful position to influence the next generation.

OVERSEAS MINISTRY

- Reaching women and children in Iraq through schools and women's centers
- Training Indian women to reach women in India through Indian women's training centers
- Unreached people outreach throughout India
- Teaching literacy, study skills and evangelism to the poorest Indian women, the Dalits
- Microloans for women in Afghanistan
- Training Chinese leaders in house churches (75% of new believers in these churches are women)
- Education for girls in China
- School and life programs for China's HIV/AIDS orphans
- Outreach in North Korea
- Community development and wholistic outreach in North Africa, village by village
- Training Arab women for ministry
- Training and outreach in Northern Sumatra
- Job training and work programs in Sudan for displaced women

If you'd like to strengthen the weak and speak up for the voiceless, please contact:

Sisters In Service
www.SistersInService.org